CAKE
BOI

CAKE BOI

A Collection of Classic Bakes

by **REECE HIGNELL**

MasterChef Australia Finalist
and Founder of Cakeboi Bakery

PAGE STREET
PUBLISHING CO.

PAGE STREET
PUBLISHING CO.

First published in 2022 by
Page Street Publishing Co.
27 Congress Street, Suite 1511
Salem, MA 01970
www.pagestreetpublishing.com

Distributed by Macmillan, sales in Canada by The Canadian Manda Group.

26   25   24   23   22   1   2   3   4   5

ISBN-13: 978-1-64567-576-1
ISBN-10: 1-64567-576-9

Library of Congress Control Number: 2022930187

Cover and book design by Kylie Alexander for Page Street Publishing Co.
Cover art by Dene Whitfield
Photography by Luisa Brimble
Shoot arts and styling by Zoë Lonergan

Printed and bound in China

Page Street Publishing protects our planet by donating to nonprofits like The Trustees, which focuses on local land conservation.

This book is wholeheartedly dedicated to my nan,
Heather Bates. Writing this book has filled me with joy,
remembering the baking fairy tale of my childhood.

Admittedly, it took me a long time to truly appreciate
your baking as much as I do now, sadly a little too late.
But with these recipes your memory will live on forever.

Table of Contents

Foreword

When it comes to being part of *MasterChef Australia* history, Reece Hignell knows that sensation better than I do; he's been a beloved part of it since season 10! When we met a few years later—I in my first season as judge and he returning as a contestant on *Back to Win*—we talked about what had changed in the time he'd been away from the show. He said that his first time was fun, but he didn't then feel truly comfortable being all of himself in that kitchen and in front of the world—and who can blame him?

He returned, though, with a discernible change in perspective. There was a clear sense of owning himself unapologetically and celebrating his own unique and truly special sense of identity. That realness (and, frankly, often silliness!) is something I valued in Reece from the second we met: There really is something to be said for being around a person who accepts himself in all his inspiring, beautiful work-in-progress glory.

Perhaps one of the most real things about Reece is his love of properly good, old-school (and therefore wonderful) cake. The retro nostalgia is strong with this human, and I bloody love him for it! From his nan's passionfruit sponge to classic tarts, biscuits and other recipes filled with shared memory, warmth and approachable skill, this book is all about an amped-up sense of feel-good factor. And yes, it even contains Reece's very fabulous lemon tart—and the babas that made Katy Perry fold a napkin into boobs and call Reece "the tits." It's a moment I'll never forget, and I suspect that it will live rent free in the hearts and minds of *MC* fans for the rest of time.

Pastry can be difficult, but it can also be comforting, creative and, as Reece likes to say, "cute." So when you're looking for things to make that are the culinary equivalent of a hug, a wave or a little soothing balm for the woes of the world, you could do worse than to start right here.

Call him Cakeboi, Doll or the retro cake specialist, to me—and Katy Perry—Reece and his sweet creations will always be "the tits."

—Melissa Leong

MasterChef Australia Judge, Food Writer

Introduction

Hey guys, I'm Reece.

Once upon a time, I auditioned for the world's most popular reality cooking show, *MasterChef*. I was always a fan of the show, and finally I decided to be a real whisk taker and audition, batter late than never! I was just a self-taught home baker with a passion for cooking, and suddenly I was on TV battling the odds against 50 contestants. Spoiler alert, I didn't win, but top 6 was still a huge achievement. After that season, I left my office job and followed my passion. I started working in the food industry and developed my interest in baking. My motto is "Life is what you bake of it."

In 2020, I was back, back, back again to win! This time, I was asked to return for an all-stars version. I competed against *MasterChef Australia*'s finest and I finished as a lovely fifth alternate.

After leaving the show, by the power vested in me—by me—I decided to start my own business known as Cakeboi. In a fast-paced culinary world where everyone is looking to be innovative, creative and unique, I decided to take a step back; I took inspiration from my nan's recipes and created an old-school cake shop. When I was growing up, she had a weekly market stall jam-packed full of cakes. She was the Marie Antoinette of Warners Bay's, New South Wales, Australia, who provided the goods and let them eat cake. She sold an abundance of cakes, including her amazing passionfruit sponge, the humble carrot cake and those showstopping scones. Many of her recipes are found in this book and used at my shop, and now you too will be able to make them.

Classic Aussie bakes have stolen my heart and are the essence of Cakeboi. Now it's time to pass on Nan's legacy, from her, to me, to you. So grab your bowl and whisk, because all you'll need is this book to create some old-school beautiful bakes.

Happy baking!

Things to Know
Before You Start

Eggs

Eggs are so important for baking. They add richness in flavor and levelling in rise, and they help the stability of your baked goods, so selecting the right egg is essential.

First and foremost, when baking a cake, always use a fresh free-range egg. This is especially important when whipping the egg, as fresh eggs aerate better. Of course free range is crucial, as the quality of the egg is so much better when the chicken—the "chook," as Nan would say—is provided with a better-quality life.

If you are very particular about the size of your egg, an average "large" egg weighs about 50 grams without the shell, of which approximately 20 grams is yolk and 30 grams white. So if the recipe asks for 2 eggs, then you will need 100 grams of egg.

Finally, most recipes will call for room-temperature eggs. Adding a cold egg would risk seizing any emulsified mixtures.

Butter

Butter is also central to baking, and selecting the correct butter is very important. Butter ranges from salted to unsalted and from low to high water content. So what determines the correct one?

In the debate between salted and unsalted butter, my preference always goes to salted. The amount of salt in the butter is purely to add flavor. I don't believe that it affects the end result of a cake. I know I've never noticed an overly salty cake due to using salted butter.

I would always recommend the use of a premium-grade butter, particularly when making pastry. The steam from its higher water content will help create an even more flaky result in your rough puff. The flavor of a premium butter is also very helpful when making buttercreams. It adds a beautiful richness. If you do wish to use a lower-grade butter, I would recommend using it whilst baking the actual cake.

Finally, I try to specify the temperature of the butter to be used in each recipe, but I generally suggest baking with room-temperature butter unless specified.

Caster Sugar

Caster sugar, sometimes called superfine sugar or baker's sugar, is preferred in many recipes, as it is finer than ordinary granulated sugar and dissolves more readily. It can be made by pulsing granulated sugar in a food processor for a few seconds. Granulated sugar can substitute for caster sugar gram-for-gram, but the volume needed will be increased by about 10 percent.

Icing Sugar Mixture

Icing sugar mixture is a product that we use religiously at Cakeboi when making various icings and baked goods. I will always harp on about it because it makes baking so much easier. I'm all about hassle-free methods.

Icing sugar mixture is made up of pure icing sugar (powdered sugar or confectioner's sugar) mixed with 3 percent cornstarch (called cornflour or Maizena® in many places). The added cornstarch prevents rocks of icing sugar from forming, which means you don't need to sift your sugar.

Caramelized Condensed Milk

Caramelized condensed milk is a baker's delight and so easy to make. Just place a tin of condensed milk in a saucepan, add water to cover by an inch or two (2.5 or 5 cm), bring to a boil and simmer for 3 hours. Check the water level periodically and add boiling water as needed to keep the tin submerged. When done, remove the tin with tongs, set it on a folded towel or a rack and allow it to cool thoroughly at room temperature or in the fridge before opening.

This preparation is a shortcut version of Latin America's dulce de leche, a painstaking reduction of milk and sugar. Tins of dulce de leche may nowadays be found in many food markets.

Passionfruit Pulp

In Australia, we have a passion for passionfruit, and it stars in several Cakeboi recipes, imparting a welcome tartness and a heady tropical aroma. While frozen passionfruit "pulp" is commercially available, it is watery and lacks the fruit's seeds, which give your pastry an extra crunch. Choose passionfruit that are nicely wrinkled, indicating ripeness. Slice them in half and scoop out the contents, seeds and all. One passionfruit will yield about 2 tablespoons (30 ml) of luscious pulp.

Self-Rising Flour

Many recipes call for self-rising flour. If you don't have any or can't find it, you can easily make it. For each cup of self-rising flour that you need, sift together 1 cup (125 g) of all-purpose flour, 1½ teaspoons (7 g) of baking powder and ¼ teaspoon of salt. *Et voilà*, as Aussies say.

Whisking Peaks

Throughout the book, you will see that I mention different sorts of peaks when whisking. Here is an explanation of each peak that is used in my recipes.

Soft peaks are formed by whisking cream or egg white until it can just hold its shape. The mixture will cling to the whisk, and the gentle peaks you create will fall back onto themselves. This texture is best for when folding meringues or creams into other mixtures.

Firm peaks are formed by whisking the cream or egg white until it proudly stands tall. When you lift your whisk out of the mixture, the peak that will form on the whisk will not fall onto itself. This texture is best for layering a cake or for piping.

Weighing Ingredients

A common issue with ingredients is whether to measure them by volume or by weight—cups or grams. I won't ramble on here. Invest in a good digital scale. Scales are fairly inexpensive and will make your baking life a whole lot easier. The accuracy you will introduce to your baking will pay off in the long run. If you do not own a scale and/or decide to measure by volume, the cups used in my recipes are American cups.

Oven Temperature

Another good investment is an accurate oven thermometer. Your oven may not be delivering the temperature you have selected.

Some recipes give the oven temperature with the specification "fan forced," for a convection oven. If you are using a conventional oven, the temperature will need to be 25 to 30°F (about 15°C) higher, with the baking time unchanged.

Temperature of Ingredients

Always have ingredients at room temperature unless the recipe specifies otherwise. Eggs, butter and even milk need to be at room temperature to create the most cohesive cake batter.

Preventing Pastry Leaks

When preparing a tart with a runny filling like a lemon tart, brush the inside of the tart shell with a mixture of flour and egg white. Do this when it is still hot, fresh out of the oven. This will fill any tiny gaps and cracks so that your filling does not leak from the shell. To make this mixture, just whisk together 2 parts egg white and 1 part all-purpose flour.

Mastering the Basics

If you're scared of making pastry, this is your chance to face your fears and conquer them. So if you find a recipe in this book that appeals to you, MAKE IT! Follow my directions step by step for your best chance to perfect the pastry, but be aware that achieving perfection is about understanding the feel and touch of pastry. If it doesn't work, keep trying. As they say, practice makes perfect.

1. Basic Bakes

Baking is a creative science. It relies heavily on some basic fundamentals of the baking process. A good baker understands the everyday science of a kitchen. Once you understand how each action affects the finished product, you will be able to replicate recipes easily.

Most baked goods are made of the same ingredients: flour, water, salt, fat and leavening agents. Often the only difference lies within how the ingredients are assembled or the ratios used. These small changes have a large impact on the quality of the end product. This is why it is so important to follow each recipe exactly as it is written.

This chapter contains bold baking basics, recipes that should be in the repertoire of every baker. These are the foundational building blocks you need in order to become a baking superstar. The Go-To Sweet Pastry Crust (page 18) is a must; you will use this recipe for so many things. Warning, once you make my homemade jam (page 30), you will never buy store bought again! These recipes will build your confidence so you can bake anything, anywhere!

Go-To Sweet Pastry Crust

Makes one tart shell up to 12 inches (30 cm) in diameter or two 8-inch (20-cm) tart shells

Now, I'm about to let you in on a little secret. This recipe is a staple in my baking; I use it as the base for everything. You can use this recipe as your personal cheat sheet. It is tasty, versatile and reliable. Want to spice things up? No problem, the flavoring of this pastry can easily be changed with orange zest or by replacing the vanilla with tonka bean. But be sure you follow the extra steps to prevent shrinkage. When it comes to baking, size matters!

2 cups (250 g) all-purpose flour

½ cup (110 g) unsalted butter, cold

½ cup (110 g) caster sugar

Pinch of salt

1 egg

Zest of 1 lemon

1 tsp vanilla extract

Place the flour, butter, sugar and salt in a food processor. (If you don't have a food processor, you can use a stand mixer or even a bowl and a wooden spoon. Machines just make things easier.) Process these ingredients for a few seconds until the mixture resembles breadcrumbs. Add the egg, zest and vanilla, then process again until a dough is formed. Turn the dough out onto a lightly floured surface and knead it to form a round flat disk about 1 inch (2.5 cm) thick. Wrap the dough in cling wrap, then place it in the fridge to chill until it is firm, about 2 hours.

Remove the dough from the fridge. Oil a tart tin lightly to ensure the shell does not stick. Now lightly flour your work surface and a rolling pin. Work the dough with your hands for about three (really light) kneads to ensure it is pliable enough to roll. Carefully roll the dough, turning it 90 degrees every few rolls. This helps keep the pastry consistent in its thickness. Work carefully but quickly, as you do not want the butter in the dough to soften.

Once the pastry is about ⅛ inch (3 mm) thick, carefully roll it onto your rolling pin to transport it onto your tin. Unroll the pastry over the tin and lightly ease it into the edges of the tin, ensuring there are no pockets of air under the pastry or in the flutes (if using a fluted tin). Using a sharp knife, trim the excess pastry from the rim. Chill the pastry in the freezer for about 30 minutes, or until it is firm. This will help prevent shrinkage.

(continued)

Go-To Sweet Pastry Crust (Continued)

When you're ready to bake the tart shell, preheat the oven to 355°F (180°C). Scrunch and then unscrunch a sheet of baking paper and lay it over the bottom and up the sides of the pastry. Now fill it with baking weights or beans (uncooked), ensuring that they are firmly pushed into the corners. Place the pastry in the oven and bake it for 10 minutes. Remove the baking paper and weights, then bake for an additional 10 minutes. The pastry shell should now be golden all over.

Now, the shell can of course be made up to 2 days ahead of time. However, ensure that it is stored in an airtight container away from any moisture. Alternatively, you can freeze the unbaked shell in its tin. When you're ready to bake it, it can be baked from frozen; it will just take a few minutes longer.

Almond Pastry Crust

Makes one tart shell up to 12 inches (30 cm) in diameter or two 8-inch (20-cm) tart shells

1¼ cups (160 g) all-purpose flour

½ cup (110 g) caster sugar

¾ cup (100 g) almond meal

½ cup (115 g) butter

1 egg yolk

This is an essential basic recipe for your repertoire. It is simple and quick to make, it rolls beautifully and you will definitely notice the aromatic addition on your palate. This fragrant pastry is just delicious. You can use it in place of any plain old pastry for a sweet pie or tart. It could also be filled with crème pâtissière and topped with berries, like a little French bakery tart. Your options are endless.

To make this pastry I would usually use a food processor, but you can always follow these steps with a bowl and a wooden spoon.

Firstly, combine your flour, caster sugar, almond meal and butter in a food processor and pulse it until a breadcrumb-like mixture forms. Add the egg, then pulse until the dough comes together. Transfer it to a clean work surface. Press the dough into a firm disk, wrap it in cling wrap and refrigerate it until it is firm. This should take at least 30 minutes.

Remove the dough from the fridge. Oil a fluted tart tin lightly to ensure the shell does not stick. Lightly flour your work surface and a rolling pin. This dough can become warm very quickly, so try not to overhandle it. Carefully roll the dough, turning it every few rolls, which will help keep the pastry consistent in its thickness.

Once the pastry is ⅛ inch (3 mm) thick, carefully roll it onto your rolling pin to transport it onto your tin. Unroll the pastry over the tin and lightly ease it into the edges of the tin, ensuring there are no pockets of air under the pastry or in the flutes. Using a sharp knife, trim the excess pastry from the rim. Chill the pastry in the freezer for about 30 minutes, or until it is firm. This will help prevent shrinkage.

When you are ready to bake the tart shell, preheat the oven to 355°F (180°C). Scrunch and then unscrunch a sheet of baking paper and lay it over the bottom and up the sides of the pastry. Fill it with baking weights or beans (uncooked), ensuring that they are firmly pushed into the corners. Place the pastry in the oven and bake it for 10 minutes. Remove the baking paper and weights, then bake for an additional 10 minutes. The pastry shell should now be golden all over.

Now, the shell can of course be made up to 2 days ahead of time. However, ensure that it is stored in an airtight container away from any moisture.

Chocolate Pastry Crust

Makes one tart shell up to 12 inches (30 cm) in diameter or two 8-inch (20-cm) tart shells

Making your own pastry might seem intimidating, but trust me, it is actually much easier than it seems! Have you ever thought, how do you make pastry better? The answer is, make it chocolate.

1⅔ cups (200 g) all-purpose flour

⅔ cup (150 g) butter

⅓ cup (70 g) caster sugar

2 tbsp (14 g) cocoa powder

½ tsp salt

1 egg yolk

Place the flour, butter, sugar, cocoa powder and salt in a food processor. (If you don't have a food processor, you can use a stand mixer or even a bowl and a wooden spoon. Machines just make things easier.) Process these ingredients for a few seconds until the mixture resembles breadcrumbs. Add the egg yolk, and process it again until a dough is formed. Turn the dough out onto a lightly floured surface and knead it to form a round flat disk about 1 inch (2.5 cm) thick. Wrap the dough in cling wrap, then place it in the fridge to chill until it is firm, about 2 hours.

Remove the dough from the fridge. Oil a fluted tart tin lightly to ensure the shell does not stick. Lightly flour your work surface and a rolling pin. Work the dough with your hands for about three (really light) kneads to ensure the dough is pliable enough to roll. Carefully roll the dough, turning it every few rolls. This helps keep the pastry consistent in its thickness. Work carefully but quickly, as you do not want the butter in the dough to soften.

Once the pastry is about ⅛ inch (3 mm) thick, carefully roll it onto your rolling pin to transport it onto your tin. Unroll the pastry over the tin and lightly ease it into the edges of the tin, ensuring there are no pockets of air under the pastry or in the flutes. Using a sharp knife, trim the excess pastry from the rim. Chill the pastry in the freezer for about 30 minutes, or until it is firm. This will help prevent shrinkage.

When you're ready to bake the tart shell, preheat the oven to 355°F (180°C). Scrunch and then unscrunch a sheet of baking paper and lay it over the bottom and up the sides of the pastry. Now fill it with baking weights or beans (uncooked), ensuring that they are firmly pushed into the corners. Place the pastry in the oven and bake it for 8 minutes. Remove the baking paper and weights, then bake for an additional 8 minutes. It will be difficult to see the doneness of this pastry, as it is already dark, but it should feel firm to the touch.

Now, the shell can of course be made up to 2 days ahead of time. However, ensure that it is stored in an airtight container away from any moisture.

Rough Puff Pastry

Makes one tart shell up to 12 inches (30 cm) in diameter or two 8-inch (20-cm) tart shells

1⅛ cups (250 g) cold unsalted butter, diced

2 cups (250 g) all-purpose flour, plus more for dusting

1 tsp sea salt flakes

⅓ cup (80 ml) iced water

Some like it rough! This recipe is the shortcut to achieving a puff-like pastry.

A rough puff is an essential for any baker's repertoire, and I was taught how to make this by MasterChef bestie, Brendan Pang. Brendan is someone who isn't known for desserts, but he perfected the most amazing puff pastry.

This rough puff uses what I call the rollie, foldie, turnie, repeat method, which results in thin, crispy, buttery layers of delicious pastry!

To start, place the diced butter and the food processor bowl in the freezer. (If the bowl won't fit in the freezer, at least chill it well in the fridge.) Once the butter is rock solid, place it in the cold food processor bowl together with the flour and salt, and pulse until you have a rough mixture with a large crumb-like appearance. Add the iced water and continue to pulse until it is just combined. I normally pulse until the dough has formed into little pebbles the size of lentils.

Remove the dough from the food processor and transfer it to a lightly floured surface. Working quickly, gently press the dough between your fingertips so that it comes together. Shape it into a rectangle, wrap it in cling wrap and place it in the fridge to rest for 10 minutes.

(continued)

Rough Puff Pastry (Continued)

Roll 1

Once rested, unwrap the dough and turn it out onto a lightly floured work surface. Dust a rolling pin with flour as needed and roll the dough out into a rectangle of about 8 x 16 inches (20 x 40 cm). Fold the ends in so they meet in the middle. Fold again where the ends have met, to create a book fold. Give the rectangle of dough a quarter turn. Wrap with cling wrap and rest in the fridge for 10 minutes.

Roll 2

Lightly dust with flour and roll it out again to approximately 8 x 16 inches (20 x 40 cm). Repeat the folding process. Quarter turn then wrap the dough in cling wrap and rest it in the fridge for 10 minutes.

Roll 3

Repeat the rolling and folding. Again wrap the dough in cling wrap and rest it in the fridge for 10 minutes.

Now the dough is ready to be rolled out to whatever shape you wish. Try using this rough puff for the Passionfruit Custard Slice on page 112.

Tips and Tricks: When you complete each quarter turn, press your thumb into the top right corner of the dough before each fold. It will help you remember which way you are rolling the dough after you take it out of the fridge.

Basic Berry Jam

Makes two 13-ounce (375-g) jars

Come on, we all prefer the taste of "homemade" jam.

This berry jam recipe is the perfect way to use up those spare berries throughout the year. The recipe works with any berry (strawberries, blackberries, blueberries, raspberries, mulberries, etc.), so get creative! Jam is the perfect solution for berries that have just passed the point of eating. Don't throw them out! Even if they start to look withered, that's just a sign their sweetness has levelled up! Now, go and make some berry nice jam!

3–4 cups (500 g) berries of your choice

1¾ cups (375 g) sugar

1 lemon, freshly juiced

Prepare two jam jars. They need to be sterilized, so place them in a pot of boiling water for a few minutes. Use tongs to remove the jars, then set them on a clean tea towel to dry.

For the jam, first place a small plate in the freezer. Slice all the larger berries in half, then toss them in the sugar. Combine the berries, sugar and fresh lemon juice in a large pot and set it over medium heat. When the jam starts to simmer, turn the heat down so that the jam does not reach a boil. Let it simmer for 15 minutes.

Note: The hot jam creates pressure inside the jar and should be sufficient to seal the lid. This is the method Nan always used. If you prefer, you can water bath can the jars after they're filled or simply store the jars in the fridge.

To test if the jam has reached the setting point, take a small spoonful of the hot jam, dollop it onto the frozen plate and return the plate to the freezer for 1 minute. Run your finger through the jam. If the finger mark remains there, the jam is set.

Turn the heat off, then carefully transfer the jam to the two prepared jars. Now seal and label them (see Note). This jam should be stored in a cool, dry place such as the pantry and used within 1 year of making. Once opened, the jar should be kept in the refrigerator and used within one month.

Tips and Tricks: Since berries vary in weight, it's impossible to generalize about volume quantities. Just weigh them. (Indeed, for best results, weigh everything whenever you're baking anything.) You won't always have exactly half a kilo of berries, so scale the recipe: Whatever weight of berries you have, take three-quarters that weight of sugar, with lemon juice adjusted as needed. If it's berry-picking season, make a lot. Scrounge empty jars from your neighbor, and return one jar full.

Basic Buttercream

Makes enough to ice one 3- to 4-layer cake

2¼ cups (500 g) butter, softened

7 cups (960 g) icing sugar, or icing sugar mixture (page 14)

1 tbsp (15 ml) milk, at room temperature

2 tsp (10 ml) vanilla extract

Optional Flavor Additions

Orange: zest of 1 large orange

Lemon: zest of 1 lemon and 1 tbsp (15 ml) lemon juice

Chocolate: ¼ cup (25 g) cocoa powder

Mocha: ¼ cup (25 g) cocoa powder and 1 tbsp (5 g) espresso powder

Nutella: 2 cups (580 g) Nutella

Peanut butter: 2 cups (500 g) peanut butter

Buttercream is a staple in any baker's kitchen. For some, a cake is simply the vehicle for the icing. This icing is super soft, creamy and sweet. There's nothing fancy about the way it is made, but it will certainly be amazing! This buttercream icing is versatile, too; you can flavor it however you choose and use it for just about anything. It is made with just a handful of simple ingredients. Never underestimate the power of a good icing!

To make the buttercream, first you need to ensure that your butter is softened but not melted. I like to use softened butter, as it creates a super smooth buttercream. If you're after a stiffer buttercream for piping, then just don't let the butter get too soft. If the butter is still firm, microwave it for 10 seconds to soften. Place your butter in a large metal bowl. With an electric mixer fitted with a paddle attachment, beat the butter until it turns very pale.

Sift the icing sugar into a large bowl. Turn the speed of the mixer to low, then begin to feed the icing sugar into the butter in four separate batches. Scrape down the sides after each addition, and make sure each cup is fully incorporated before adding the next one.

Add the room-temperature milk and the vanilla to the buttercream, then continue to beat it for another 2 minutes. This will smooth out the buttercream and make it nice and creamy. Once the buttercream is made, you can beat in your optional flavors on a medium speed for 1 minute.

Tips and Tricks: You can always make this buttercream well ahead and leave it in the fridge for up to a week. Just bring it back to room temperature, then beat for 2 minutes until it is smooth and creamy.

Swiss Meringue Buttercream

Makes enough to ice one 3- to 4-layer cake

White vinegar

2 cups (440 g) caster sugar

7 egg whites

3⅓ cups (750 g) butter, cubed, at room temperature

2 tsp (10 ml) vanilla extract

This stable icing is creamy and silky smooth, pipes beautifully and holds its shape well. Once you try Swiss meringue buttercream, you'll use it on everything! This Swiss meringue buttercream is my favorite of the meringue icings because it is neither overly sweet nor difficult to make.

Another benefit of Swiss meringue buttercream is that it keeps well overnight at room temperature without drying out. Therefore, you can completely assemble your cake ahead of time without taking up space in the refrigerator. It will taste just as good the next day!

Choose a heatproof bowl and rub the inside with white vinegar to remove any fat. Place your caster sugar and egg whites (ensuring that there are no yolk bits) in the bowl and set it over a medium saucepan of simmering water. As it is slowly heating, lightly whisk the egg whites until all the sugar is dissolved. I have a digital thermometer, so I bring the eggs to 140°F (60°C) and hold it at this temperature for 3 minutes. This will pasteurize the eggs.

Remove the egg whites from the heat, then whisk them with an electric mixer on a high speed until firm peaks form. The meringue should look light and pillowy, and the side of the bowl should be cool to the touch.

At this stage, I switch to a paddle attachment and reduce the speed to medium. Begin to feed the room-temperature butter in, one cube at a time. If you add the butter before the meringue is fully cooled and the butter melts, just cool the mixture in the refrigerator, then re-whip once cooled. The mixture may start to curdle, but keep beating it and it will smooth out. Ensure you beat it until the icing is smooth with no lumps. Add the vanilla, then beat for an additional 30 seconds.

Tips and Tricks: Excess buttercream can be frozen, then brought back to room temperature before whipping.

Pastry Cream (Crème Pâtissière)

Makes enough to fill a 10-inch (25-cm) tart shell

This is a simple yet delicious recipe for crème pâtissière (vanilla pastry cream). It is a rich, creamy vanilla custard that you can use in a variety of decadent desserts. It's also the base of many creams; in this book we use it to make the Vanilla Diplomat Cream on page 78. We use this pastry cream a lot at my bakery, Cakeboi. If you want to cheat, you can use custard powder instead of cornstarch for added flavor.

Pastry cream is another basic recipe that needs to be in every baker's repertoire. It's an easy and versatile workhorse in the baker's kitchen.

2½ cups (600 ml) pouring or light whipping cream

1 vanilla bean

6 egg yolks

⅓ cup (75 g) caster sugar

6 tbsp (50 g) cornstarch

3 tbsp (40 g) butter, cold and cubed

Firstly, pour your cream into a medium-sized pot. Halve the vanilla pod to release the seeds, and add the pod and seeds to the cream. Gently heat until the cream reaches a simmer.

In a separate heatproof bowl, whisk together your egg yolks with your caster sugar until the mixture is light and foamy. Add the cornstarch, then whisk to incorporate it.

Whilst continually whisking, carefully pour one-third of the warm cream over the yolks. This process, called tempering the eggs, will help prevent them from curdling. Once the eggs are warmed, add them to the pot with the remaining cream. Now whisk to evenly combine them.

Return the pot to a low heat and continue to whisk the mixture as it begins to thicken. As you are whisking, ensure that no lumps are caught on the bottom of the pot. Once the mixture starts to bubble, whisk it for an additional 20 seconds, then remove it from the heat.

Pour the pastry cream into a heatproof bowl and remove the vanilla pod. Whilst whisking, begin to feed the butter in, one cube at a time. Continue to whisk until all the butter is incorporated with no remaining lumps.

Cover the pastry cream with baking paper directly on the surface to prevent a skin from forming, then place it in the refrigerator to set.

This pastry cream is ready to be used as the filling for tarts or cakes.

2.
Classic Cakes

The name says it all. These vintage cakes have stood the test of time. I have always loved classic cakes, and their popularity is making a comeback. Classic cakes are more interesting. They are layered with flavor and texture, unlike your modern "mud cake." These classic gems have pleasant pockets of splendid surprises hidden within them. Whether it be the crunch of a nut or the zing from a spice, classic cakes trump all their modern successors. Nan would bake a lot of the cakes in this chapter. When I was a child, the banana cake (page 41) and the carrot cake (page 46) were among my favorites. For this reason, I have included them at my bakery, and they are some of our best sellers.

There is never a wrong opportunity for cake. Whether it is for a birthday, afternoon tea or just because you can, these versatile desserts are sure to please. So eat a slice of history and taste heaven as you bake your way through these classic cake recipes. Feel the sense of nostalgia, and make your grandma proud. These cakes deserve to be made!

Banana and Coconut Cake with Caramelized Condensed Milk Icing

Makes one 8-inch (20-cm) cake

1⅛ cups (250 g) butter, at room temperature

1 cup (220 g) caster sugar

3 eggs

3 bananas, overripe

2 cups (250 g) self-rising flour

½ cup (50 g) shredded coconut

1 tsp vanilla extract

1 tsp ground cinnamon

1 tsp ground allspice

Caramelized Condensed Milk Icing

14 oz (395 g) caramelized condensed milk (page 14)

1½ cups (350 g) butter, softened in the microwave for 10 seconds

1 cup (140 g) icing sugar

1 tsp vanilla extract

2 tbsp (12 g) shredded coconut, for decorating

This cake is something to go bananas about! The key to baking this cake is to use extra-ripe bananas to add maximum sweetness. My best friend Josh, who is also an avid baker, once told me if you see the little fruit flies buzzing around your bananas, then they are perfect for baking. As bananas ripen, they get sweeter, and you want sweet bananas to elevate the flavor of this banana cake.

Watch out, because the combination of banana, caramelized condensed milk and coconut is addictive. Ask Cakeboi's regular customer "the Fabulous Julie." She isn't a happy little monkey if we sell out of banana cake before she gets her fix.

Preheat the oven to 340°F (170°C), then grease an 8-inch (20 cm) tin and line it with baking paper. You can also use an 8-inch (20-cm) square tin, which looks great when serving this cake for morning tea.

To start this cake, place the room-temperature butter and sugar in a large bowl and beat with an electric mixer on high for 2 to 3 minutes, or until light and fluffy. Begin to add the eggs, one at a time. Ensure that you do not move on to the next egg until the first one is fully combined. Scrape down the sides, then beat for an additional 3 minutes. In a separate bowl, break up the bananas until they are a smooth paste and then fold them through the egg mixture. Sift in the flour, then add the coconut, vanilla, cinnamon and allspice and fold them through to create a smooth cake batter. Pour the mixture into the prepared tin. Place it on the middle rack of the oven and bake it for 45 minutes, or until the center of the cake is firm to the touch. Remove the cake from the oven and allow it to sit in the tin for a few minutes before turning it out onto a cooling rack.

To make the icing, place the caramelized condensed milk, butter, icing sugar and vanilla in a bowl and beat everything with an electric mixer. Start on a low speed and beat for 5 minutes until the icing is smooth and glossy.

To assemble, carefully cut the cake horizontally through the center to create two layers. Place the bottom layer on your cake stand, then dollop half the icing on the bottom layer and spread it to the edges. Place the top layer of the cake on the icing, and spread the remaining icing over the top of this new layer. Sprinkle shredded coconut around the edges of the top of the cake.

Makes one 8-inch (20-cm) cake

⅔ cup (150 g) butter

5 eggs

1⅔ cups (375 g) caster sugar

1¼ cups (310 ml) buttermilk, at room temperature

5 tsp (25 ml) liquid red food dye

2⅓ cups (300 g) self-rising flour

½ cup (50 g) cocoa powder

Cream Cheese Icing

¾ cup (172 g) butter, at room temperature

13 oz (375 g) cream cheese, at room temperature

3¼ cups (450 g) icing sugar

2 tsp (10 ml) vanilla extract

Striking, bold and captivating, red is perhaps the most dominant of colors, and this red velvet cake is no exception; it reigns as a best seller at Cakeboi. This is one attractive cake. It captures your eye with its scarlet hue and its crown of sweet but tart cream cheese icing. When eating red velvet cake, you're getting bites of fluffy, moist cake with a creamy, delicate icing that leaves your mouth feeling wonderful. No wonder it's a timeless classic!

Preheat the oven to 355°F (180°C). Line a cake tin that is 8 inches (20 cm) in diameter and about 3 inches (8 cm) high with baking paper and set it aside. I don't grease the sides for this cake, as I find that it rises better this way.

In a microwave-safe bowl, heat the butter in the microwave for 1 minute, or until melted, then set it aside until needed. Place the eggs and caster sugar in the bowl of an electric mixer and whisk them on high until thick and glossy. This may take up to 10 minutes.

In a separate bowl, mix together the melted butter, buttermilk and red food dye. The mixture may curdle a little, but just keep mixing it. Fold this buttermilk mixture into the egg mixture in three batches using a spatula. Be extra gentle, so you don't destroy all the air bubbles. Now sift the flour and cocoa powder together, then fold them through the batter in two batches.

Once the batter is fully combined, pour it into the prepared cake tin and place it in the oven for 50 to 55 minutes, or until a cake tester comes out clean. Remove the cake from the oven and let it rest in the tin for 10 minutes. Run a knife around the inside of the tin, then turn the cake out and allow it to cool completely on a wire rack.

To make the cream cheese icing, place the butter and cream cheese in the bowl of an electric mixer. On medium speed, beat the mixture for 3 minutes, or until it is light and fluffy. Turn the mixer to low and add the icing sugar and vanilla. Mix until the sugar is well combined. Transfer the icing to a piping bag with a round-tip nozzle.

To assemble, cut the cake into three even layers, and cut the dome off the top of the cake. Reserve the offcuts, as they can be crumbled for decorating later. Pipe mini Hershey's Kiss shapes of icing over the first layer of the cake until it is completely covered. Repeat this process until all three layers are covered. Now stack the layers. Crumble the offcuts and sprinkle the crumbs over the top of the cake for extra decoration.

Red Velvet Cake with Cream Cheese Icing

Cakeboi Birthday Cake

Makes one 8-inch (20-cm) cake

2¼ cups (500 g) butter, at room temperature

2 cups (440 g) caster sugar

8 eggs, at room temperature

4 tsp (20 ml) vanilla extract

3¼ cups (400 g) self-rising flour

Pinch of salt

½ cup (120 g) sour cream

1 serving Swiss Meringue Buttercream (page 34)

1 serving strawberry Basic Berry Jam (page 30)

4 drops light pink food gel

½ cup (100 g) sprinkles

Hip hip, HOORAY! For a festive occasion, nothing compares to the spirit of a classic birthday cake. Celebrate in style by baking Cakeboi's simple but stunning sour cream butter cake. This flavorsome party starter is plush, soft and moist. It is suitable for any occasion because this diverse recipe can be baked as a slab or a stacked cake. Don't forget the sprinkles for that Funfetti® birthday vibe. May the birthday person rejoice in the magic of a meaningful moment when cutting this delicious dessert.

Preheat the oven to 340°F (170°C) and prepare two 8-inch (20-cm) baking tins with baking paper on the bottom of the tins. I don't grease the sides for this cake, as I find that it rises better this way.

To start the cake, beat the room-temperature butter and sugar together with an electric mixer until the mixture is thick and pale. This can take 2 to 3 minutes. On a medium speed, add the eggs one at a time. Do not add the next egg until the previous egg is fully incorporated. Add the vanilla extract and beat the mixture for an additional 2 minutes until it is light and creamy. Scrape down the sides of the bowl, then mix again for another 30 seconds.

Sift the flour and salt onto the mixture and gently fold it through, then fold in the sour cream. Pour this batter into the prepared tins and place them on the middle rack of the oven. Bake for 40 to 45 minutes, or until the center of the cake is firm to the touch. Remove the cakes from the oven and leave them in the tins until completely cooled.

Prepare the Swiss Meringue Buttercream as per page 34. Remove half the icing mixture and fold the strawberry jam through it. Add the food gel to the remaining white icing and fold it though. This will create a strawberry icing for between the layers and a pink icing for the exterior.

Cut each cake into two even layers, leaving you with four layers total. Begin to ice the cake by placing the bottom layer on a cake stand and evenly spreading one-third of the strawberry icing over the layer. Repeat this process until all the layers are stacked. Run an offset spatula around the outside of the cake to smooth the icing, then place it in the fridge to firm.

Remove the cake from the fridge and cover the exterior with the pink icing. Now decorate the cake with sprinkles, then place it back in the fridge to set firm.

Makes one 8-inch (20-cm) cake

This recipe is easy to make, versatile and utterly delicious. At Cakeboi it is one of our most popular cakes, because it is sweetly spiced, super moist and smothered with velvety cream cheese icing. I believe it is truly the best carrot cake, the cake that sets the standard for carrot cakes everywhere. Its vibrant flavor comes from the brown sugar and spices that are added to the carrots. The cake is dense, yet still surprisingly soft and lush. The best thing about this cake is that the flavor intensifies over time and the cream cheese icing seeps into the layers, creating an even more tender bite.

2⅓ cups (300 g) all-purpose flour

2 tsp (10 g) baking powder

1 tsp baking soda

2 tsp (6 g) ground cinnamon

1 tsp ground allspice

1 tsp ground nutmeg

1 cup (235 g) brown sugar

1 cup (225 g) raw sugar

4 eggs

1 cup (240 ml) vegetable oil

3 cups (375 g) finely grated carrot

2 cups (200 g) chopped walnuts or pecans

1 cup (100 g) shredded coconut

Brown Butter, Honey and Cream Cheese Icing

¾ cup (175 g) butter

18 oz (500 g) cream cheese, at room temperature

½ cup (120 ml) honey

1 cup (100 g) toasted walnuts or pecans, finely chopped

Preheat the oven to 340°F (170°C). Grease an 8-inch (20-cm) cake tin that is about 3 inches (8 cm) high, and line the base with baking paper.

To start this cake, sift together the flour, baking powder, baking soda, cinnamon, allspice and nutmeg. In a separate bowl, with an electric mixer with a whisk attachment, whisk the two sugars, eggs and oil on a high speed for about 5 minutes, or until light and fluffy.

Gently fold the flour mixture through the whisked mixture, ensuring that you don't deflate the eggs. Add the carrot, chopped walnuts and shredded coconut, then fold them in to create a smooth, light batter. Pour the mixture into the prepared tin, then place it on the middle rack of the oven and bake for 1¼ hours, or until the center of the cake is firm to the touch. Remove the cake from the oven and allow it to sit in the tin for a few minutes before turning it out onto a cooling rack.

For the icing, first prepare the brown butter: Set your butter in a saucepan over medium heat until it melts and slowly comes to a boil. The butter will begin to foam; constantly stir it, as the milk solids will cling to the bottom of the pan. Cook the butter until the milk solids begin to caramelize and release a nutty aroma. Pour the butter into a mixing bowl and allow it to cool to room temperature.

Add the cream cheese and honey to the brown butter, then using an electric mixer with a paddle attachment, beat the icing until smooth. Stop the mixer as soon as you have a smooth icing, as you do not want to overbeat the cream cheese.

To assemble the cake, carefully cut the cake horizontally through the center to create two layers. Place the bottom layer on your cake stand, then dollop one-third of the icing on the bottom layer and spread to the edges. Place the top layer on the icing, then spread the remaining icing over the top, and down the sides of the cake and smooth out the surfaces. Carefully press the chopped toasted walnuts around the outside of the cake to decorate.

The Humble
Carrot Cake

Devil's Food Cake aka Chocolate Lover's Heaven

Makes one 8-inch (20-cm) cake

3¾ cups (480 g) all-purpose flour

3⅛ cups (700 g) caster sugar

1¾ cups (170 g) cocoa powder

4 tsp (18 g) baking soda

1 tsp baking powder

1 tbsp (18 g) salt

1 tsp ground nutmeg

2 cups (480 ml) milk

1 cup (240 ml) vegetable oil

2 tsp (10 ml) vanilla extract

4 eggs

2 cups (480 ml) boiling water, left off the heat for 3 minutes after the boil

Whipped Chocolate Ganache Icing

14 oz (400 g) bittersweet chocolate (I use 54%)

2½ cups (600 ml) thickened cream or whipping cream

¼ cup (50 g) butter

1 tsp vanilla extract

Pinch of salt

You have to try this sinfully delicious recipe for Devil's Food Cake! It's an old-fashioned recipe that's exploding with rich flavor. It's moist yet dense, and totally decadent! The creamy chocolate ganache icing is luscious, and it's the perfect finish for this beautiful cake. Forget its sinful name; this cake is heavenly.

Preheat the oven to 320°F (160°C) fan forced, or, for a non-convection oven, 345°F (175°C). Grease two 8-inch (20-cm) cake tins and line them with baking paper.

In a large mixing bowl, sift the flour, caster sugar, cocoa powder, baking soda, baking powder, salt and nutmeg then place to the side. In the bowl of a stand mixer, mix together the milk, vegetable oil, vanilla extract and eggs with a paddle attachment, on a medium speed for 1 minute.

Add the dry ingredients into the wet one third at a time, fully combining each addition before moving onto the next. Once fully incorporated, add the boiling water then mix for an additional 1 minute.

Divide the mixture between the two cake tins then place them into the oven to bake for 50 to 55 minutes, or until you're able to insert a skewer into the center and it comes out clean. For this cake, a few moist crumbs are okay. Place cake on a wire rack to cool for 30 minutes before turning the cakes out.

For the icing, finely chop the chocolate, then place it into a heatproof bowl. Pour the thickened cream into a saucepan and heat it until the cream reaches a simmer. Add the butter then pour the heated cream over the chopped chocolate. Let it sit for 1 minute before stirring it. Mix the cream through the chocolate to ensure everything is smooth and glossy. Now, add the vanilla and salt and stir to combine it all. Place it in the refrigerator for 1 hour to set.

With an electric mixer fitted with a paddle attachment, beat the icing until it reaches soft peaks.

To assemble this cake, horizontally cut each cake into two layers creating four total cake layers, then cut the dome tops of the top layers to level each layer out. Save these offcuts for use in decorating, if desired. Place the bottom layer of the cake onto your cake stand then generously spread the icing over the first layer. Repeat this process, stack the cakes then spread the icing over the top of the cake and around the sides. If you want to use the offcuts, crumble up the remaining cake then scatter it around the sides of the icing.

Basque Cheesecake

Makes one 8-inch (20-cm) cake

2.2 lb (1 kg) cream cheese

1 cup (220 g) caster sugar

6 eggs

2⅛ cups (500 ml) pouring or light whipping cream

⅓ cup (40 g) all-purpose flour

2 tbsp (30 ml) sweet sherry

1½ tsp (8 ml) vanilla extract

½ tsp ground nutmeg (optional)

Do you have a habit of burning your food? Perfect! This recipe is for you, then. This cheesecake should be burnt, cracked and cooked at high heat; therefore, it's impossible to mess up.

The first Basque cheesecake was created at La Viña in San Sebastián. Over the years, this rustic dessert has become a worldwide phenomenon. The Basque cheesecake is often called "burnt" cheesecake due to its iconic rich dark surface. Unlike American cheesecake, Basque cheesecake does not have a crust.

This cake is so interesting. It is golden and caramelized on the outside and soft and creamy in the center. You bake it on an incredible hot heat to burn (basque) the cheesecake. This high temperature forms a caramelized exterior that serves as a natural crust for the cheesecake. As it cools and sets, it deflates and creates the most amazing taste.

Burn, baby, burn!

Preheat the oven to 390°F (200°C). Prepare an 8-inch (20-cm) springform baking tin with baking paper lining the base and sides of the tin. Ensure the baking paper rises a good inch (2.5 cm) above the lip of the tin, as this cake will rise.

To start the cake, place the cream cheese and the caster sugar in a large mixing bowl. With an electric mixer fitted with a paddle attachment, beat it on a medium speed for 5 minutes. Now begin to add the eggs, one egg at a time. Do not move on to the next egg until the previous egg is fully incorporated. Beat the mixture for an additional 2 minutes to smooth out any lumps.

Fold in the cream, flour, sherry, vanilla and nutmeg until a smooth, thick cake batter is formed. Pour the batter into the prepared cake tin, then place it in the preheated oven for 55 minutes.

Remove the cake from the oven. It should be caramelized with a dark top, but still have a soft jiggle in the middle. Leave the cake on a cooling rack to cool to room temperature before placing it in the fridge for 2 hours to set firm.

Classic Ricotta Cheesecake

**Makes one 8-inch
(20-cm) cake**

This baked ricotta cheesecake is similar in style to the American cheesecake. However, the ricotta cheese filling is incredibly light, fluffy and heavenly. Unlike most patisserie cakes, this one is surprisingly low in sugar, too.

A lot of people prefer a no-bake cheesecake, but this one is well worth trying something new. We use a water bath to bake this cheesecake, which ensures the cake does not overcook and become too firm. This cheesecake is seriously addictive, a real crowd pleaser and it will leave everyone craving more!

1 (9-oz [250-g]) packet ginger nut biscuits, see Tips and Tricks

7 tbsp (100 g) butter, melted

Pinch of salt

18 oz (500 g) cream cheese

½ cup (110 g) caster sugar

4 eggs

1 cup (250 g) smooth ricotta

1 tsp vanilla extract

Zest of 1 lemon, orange or grapefruit

2 cups (300 g) fresh berries

1 tbsp (18 g) Basic Berry Jam (page 30)

Preheat the oven to 320°F (160°C) fan forced, or, for a non-convection oven, 345°F (175°C). Grease an 8-inch (20-cm) springform tin and line it with baking paper. Boil a kettle full of water. You will also need a deep baking dish that is big enough for your tin to fit into.

Lay some aluminum foil on the countertop, then place your cake tin in the center. Ensure you have a good 1½ inches (4 cm) extra up the sides of the tin the whole way around. Press the foil up the sides of the tin, ensuring that there are no gaps in the foil. Your tin will sit in a water bath, so it is important to seal in the springform tin.

Place the ginger biscuits in a ziplock bag, then crush them by rolling a rolling pin over the bag to create a fine crumb. Transfer the crushed biscuits to a bowl, add the melted butter and salt, then mix them through. Using the base of a jar or a tumbler glass, press the crumb into the base of the tin, allowing about 1 inch (2.5 cm) of crumb to come up the sides. Place in the fridge for at least 3 hours or up to overnight to firm.

Now place your cream cheese in a large mixing bowl. With an electric mixer fitted with a paddle attachment, beat the cream cheese on a medium speed for 1 minute. Add the sugar, then one egg at a time, not moving on to the next until the previous egg is fully incorporated. Add the ricotta, vanilla and citrus zest, then beat for an additional 1 minute.

Pour the cream cheese mixture into the cake tin, then jiggle the tin to even it out. Place your baking tray in the oven, pour in your boiled water until it comes up at least a scant 1 inch (2.5 cm), then carefully place your foil-clad cheesecake tin in the water. Bake for 45 to 50 minutes, or until the edges are set and there is a slight jiggle in the center. Remove the cheesecake from the water bath and allow it to cool to room temperature, then place it in the refrigerator for 3 hours to set.

Before serving, toss the berries in the jam, then scatter them over the top of the cheesecake.

Tips and Tricks:
Australian "ginger nut" biscuits, which contain no nuts, are much like American ginger snaps. In this recipe they can be replaced with arrowroot biscuits.

The Boozy-Misu

Serves 8

I love tiramisu because it has all the best things in one sweet little package: coffee, brandy, creamy custard and chocolate!

1 serving Versatile Vanilla Sponge Cake (page 63)

1¼ cups (300 ml) strong coffee or espresso

6 egg yolks

1 cup (200 g) sugar

2 oz (60 ml) brandy

Zest of 1 orange

2 cups (500 g) mascarpone

2 cups (480 ml) thickened or whipping cream

¼ cup (25 g) dark cocoa powder

Tiramisu has a marvellous mascarpone filling layered with lovely ladyfingers that have been soaked in a quality espresso mixture of your choice and finally dusted with a hint of cocoa powder. At Cakeboi we create this dessert with our locally roasted coffee, "Floozy." We love to support local businesses, and we believe that quality product always creates an even more magnificent cake. This liqueur dessert will warm you up this winter and is sure to be a crowd pleaser.

To start, prepare your Versatile Vanilla Sponge Cake in a 12 x 16-inch (30 × 40-cm) baking tray, the same as you would for the Swiss roll on page 67. Once it is cooked, drop the temperature of the oven to 250°F (120°C) for an additional 20 minutes to dry the sponge out. Now you can cut it into individual ladyfingers about 1 x 2½ inches (2.5 × 6 cm).

Brew your coffee. Stronger is better for this recipe. Instant coffee is fine, but at Cakeboi we just use espresso.

Place your egg yolks, sugar, brandy and orange zest in a large heatproof bowl, then whisk them immediately to combine them all. Place the bowl over a large pot of boiling water, and continually whisk the egg mixture whilst it thickens. This might take as many as 8 to 10 minutes.

Remove the bowl from the heat, then add the mascarpone. Whisk until it is smooth and glossy. Place it in the fridge until it is needed. In a large bowl, whip your cream with an electric mixer with a whisk attachment until it forms soft peaks. Begin to fold this cream through your mascarpone mixture until all the cream is evenly incorporated.

To assemble, firstly choose your serving dish; an 8 x 12-inch (20 x 30-cm) casserole dish will accommodate the ladyfingers in two layers, but you can use whatever you'd like (or whatever you've got). Quickly submerge the ladyfingers, one at a time, in the coffee, then cover the base of the serving dish with half of them. Spoon half of your mascarpone cream mixture onto the layer of soaked fingers. Repeat with another layer of soaked ladyfingers and the rest of the mascarpone. Dust the top with the dark cocoa powder, then place the dish in the refrigerator for at least 5 hours or overnight to set.

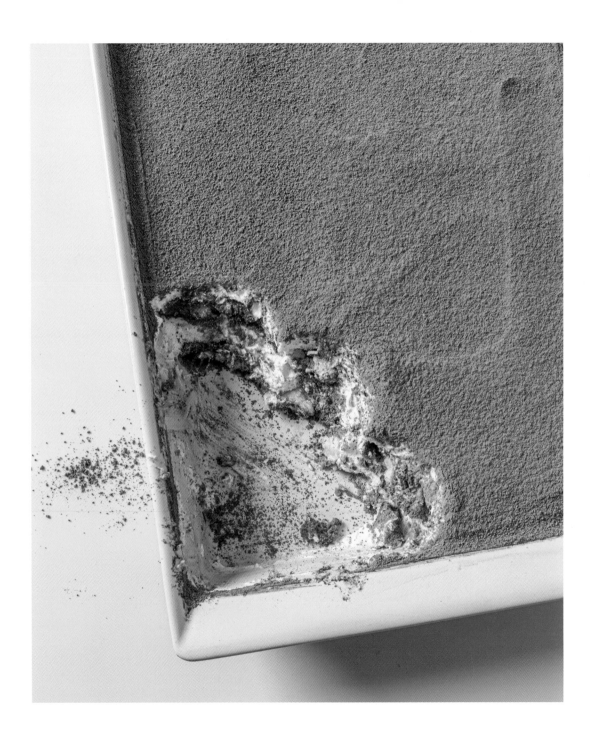

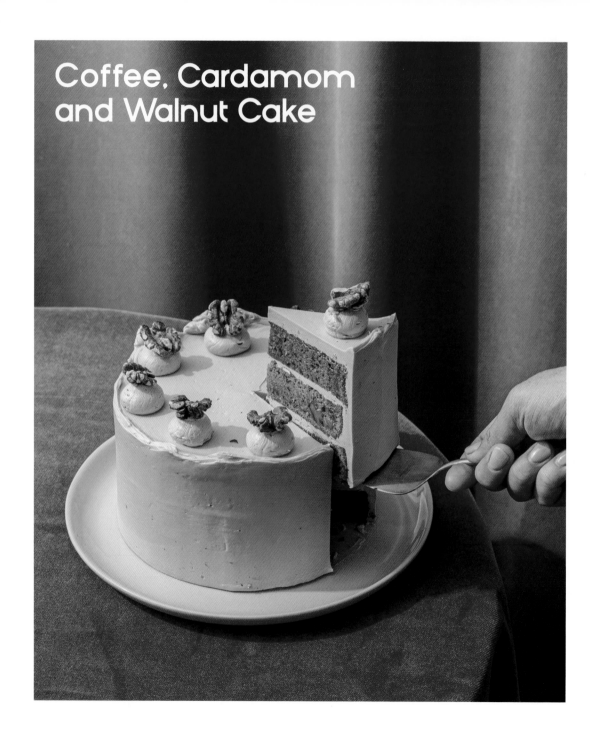

Coffee, Cardamom and Walnut Cake

Makes one 8-inch (20-cm) cake

The classic pairing of coffee and walnut is taken to a whole new tasty level in this recipe with the addition of cardamom. Cardamom complements coffee beautifully, and when mixed with walnuts it produces an extraordinary fusion that makes this cake irresistible. This delicious creation is more than just a coffee cake. It is rich and moist and packed with flavor. You'll never look at a typical boring coffee cake again, because you'll be hooked on this exciting enhancement!

2 tbsp (10 g) instant coffee

2 tbsp (30 ml) boiling water

2 cups (250 g) self-rising flour

2 cups (420 g) dark brown sugar

2 tsp (6 g) cardamom

2 cups (480 ml) pouring or light whipping cream

½ cup (120 ml) milk

4 eggs

1 tbsp (15 ml) vanilla extract

1 cup (100 g) walnuts, roughly chopped

Candied Walnuts

¼ cup (60 g) caster sugar

2 tbsp (30 ml) water

1 cup (100 g) walnut halves

½ tsp cardamom

Icing

1 tsp instant coffee

1 tsp boiling water

1 serving Caramelized Condensed Milk Icing (page 41)

Preheat the oven to 340°F (170°C) fan forced, or, for a non-convection oven, 365°F (185°C), then grease an 8-inch (20-cm) tin and line it with baking paper.

In a small bowl, mix together the instant coffee and the boiling water, then set it aside to cool. Into a large mixing bowl, sift together the flour, dark brown sugar and cardamom. In a separate bowl whisk together the pouring cream, milk, eggs and vanilla until well combined.

Gradually add the wet mixture to the dry, lightly beating the mixture with a wooden spoon. Add the walnuts and the (dissolved) instant coffee, then mix it all. Pour the cake batter into the prepared cake tin and bake for 50 to 55 minutes, or until a skewer inserted into the cake comes out clean. Turn the cake out onto a wire rack to cool.

For the candied walnuts, prepare a baking tray with baking paper. Heat the sugar and water in a small saucepan over a medium heat, stirring with a wooden spoon until the sugar starts to melt. Continue to heat for 5 to 10 minutes, or until your caramel reaches an amber color. Add the walnuts and cardamon to the pan, then stir to coat the nuts with the sugar. Pour them onto the tray, then use a fork to space them out. Cool to room temperature.

To make the icing, mix the instant coffee and the boiling water in a small bowl, then set it aside to cool to room temperature. Prepare your Caramelized Condensed Milk Icing as per page 41, then add the cooled coffee and mix to incorporate it fully.

To assemble, carefully cut the cake horizontally to create three even layers, leaving the dome attached. Place the bottom layer on your cake stand, then dollop enough icing on the layer to cover, and spread it to the edges. Add a second layer, ice it and add the top layer. Now spread most of the remaining icing around the top and sides of the cake, smoothing it out with a spatula. To ensure the candied walnuts remain on the cake, dollop or pipe more of the icing on top of the cake to create some texture for the sprinkled nuts to settle on.

Makes one 8-inch (20-cm) cake

My brothers and I would fight over Neapolitan ice cream for our favorite flavors. This cake combines all the perfectly matched flavors into one cake, so no need for fighting.

2¼ cups (500 g) butter, at room temperature

2 cups (440 g) caster sugar

8 eggs, at room temperature

4 tsp (20 ml) vanilla extract

3¼ cups (400 g) self-rising flour

Pinch of salt

½ cup (120 g) sour cream

2 tbsp (14 g) cocoa powder

¼ cup (60 g) strawberries, pureed

Pink food dye

Icing

1 serving Basic Buttercream (page 33)

1 tbsp (7 g) cocoa powder

Pink food dye

Preheat the oven to 340°F (170°C) and prepare two 8-inch (20-cm) baking tins with baking paper on the bottom of the tin. I don't grease the sides for this cake, as I find that it rises better this way.

In a large mixing bowl, beat the room-temperature butter and sugar together with an electric mixer for 2 to 3 minutes, or until it is thick and pale. On a medium speed, add the eggs one at a time, fully incorporating before adding the next egg. Add the vanilla, and beat the mixture for an additional 2 minutes until it is light and creamy. Scrape down the sides of the bowl, then mix for an additional 30 seconds.

Sift the flour and salt onto the mixture, then gently fold it through. Add the sour cream and fold it in to complete the batter.

Evenly divide the batter between three bowls. In bowl 1, sift in the cocoa powder and fold through. In bowl 2, fold through the strawberry puree plus only as much pink food dye as needed to achieve a pastel pink. Leave the third as vanilla. Spoon one color into the center of each tin, placing the next color directly on top, followed by the third color. Continue this until all the batter is in the tins. Then run a thin knife through the mixture to create a marbled effect.

Bake the tins on the middle rack for 40 to 45 minutes, or until the centers of the cakes are firm to the touch. Remove the cakes from the oven and leave them in the tins until completely cooled.

For the icing, prepare the Basic Buttercream as per page 33. Place one-quarter of the buttercream in a separate bowl, then another quarter in another bowl. In bowl 1, sift in the cocoa powder and stir until combined. In bowl 2 add pink food dye, one drop at a time until you achieve a pastel pink and stir to combine. Leave the remaining half as vanilla.

Cut each cake into two even layers, leaving the dome attached. Place a bottom layer on your cake stand, then begin to ice the cake by using the vanilla buttercream, evenly spreading the icing over the top and sides of the layer. Repeat this process, icing the second layer with pink icing, the third with brown and the top with vanilla again, until all the layers are stacked. Run an offset spatula around the outside of the cake to smooth the icing out, then place it into the fridge to firm for about 15 to 20 minutes, or until set.

Remove the cake from the fridge and cover the exterior with the remaining icing, alternating colors to make a beautiful rustic pattern.

Neapolitan
Marble
Cake

3. Superior Sponge Cakes

Visits to Nan are now treasured memories. As you entered her house, you'd hear an old Sunbeam mixer beating eggs, the sound echoing throughout the space. I remember being baffled by how unusually long she would beat these eggs for and wishing the noise would stop. Now I realize this is essential for creating the perfect sponge cake.

Nan always spoiled me with my favorite dessert—little cupcake sponges known as Fairy Cakes. As I grew, so too did my fascination with baking. I'd watch Nan pull her signature custard sponge from the oven, the aroma of passionfruit filling the air as she mixed the filling. To this day, passionfruit butter is still one of my favorite indulgences.

I believe that sponge cake is at the heart of baking. Although light and delicate, it is powerful in its impact. A sponge evokes nostalgic emotions reminiscent of loved ones.

You may recall that during *MasterChef: Back to Win*, Season 12, I made Nan's custard sponge. This was a tribute to her. I presented a worthy dish that brought a judge to tears. As Jock Zonfrillo tasted the sponge, memories of his own grandmother's classic baking flooded his heart.

In this chapter you will find recipes for an array of sponges including such favorites as Nan's Passionfruit Custard Sponge (page 71), the airy Chiffon Sponge (page 81) and Elva's Blow-Away Chocolate Sponge (page 73). My goal is for my fellow home bakers to create perfectly risen sponges fresh from the oven, so light they can be blown away by the breeze, because a failed sponge is like a breakup, the ultimate heartache.

Versatile Vanilla Sponge Cake

**Makes one 8-inch
(20-cm) cake**

6 eggs, separated

1 cup (220 g) caster sugar

1 tsp vanilla extract

1 cup (120 g) all-purpose flour

2½ tbsp (20 g) cornstarch

1 tsp baking powder

This sponge started as the first recipe from Nan's handwritten cookbook. I believe it was placed there for a reason—to set a high standard. With a few tweaks here and there we were able to make it our own. It is also unique in that it can be used for anything. At Cakeboi we make round cakes out of it, slab cakes, cut it into lamingtons and even use it for a magnificent Swiss roll.

Over the next few pages you will see the transformation of this recipe and how you can manipulate it into your very own creations.

Preheat the oven to 375°F (190°C) fan forced, or, for a non-convection oven, 400°F (205°C). Prepare two 8-inch (20-cm) baking tins by cutting baking paper into a round shape the size of the tin. Place the baking paper in the bottom of the tins, but do not grease the sides. With a sponge, I prefer not to grease the sides, so that the sponge can cling to the tin, allowing for a better rise.

With an electric mixer fitted with a whisk attachment, whisk the egg whites on a medium speed until foamy. Slowly begin to feed the sugar in, one spoon at a time, then leave the mixer running until stiff peaks form, about 8 minutes. Fold in the egg yolks and the vanilla extract. To help fold the egg yolks into the mixture, they can be lightly whisked beforehand.

Sift the flour, cornstarch and baking powder together, and then fold the dry ingredients into the egg mixture.

Divide the batter between the two tins, then place them in the oven and bake them for 18 minutes. When they come out, run a butter knife around the outside of each sponge to release it from the tin. Cool the cakes on a rack.

Using a serrated knife, trim the domed top off each cake. The pair are now ready to be used for my Strawberry and Rose Sponge Cake (page 64) or even served with just a simple layer of jam between the layers and dusted with icing sugar.

Strawberry and Rose Sponge Cake

Makes one 8-inch (20-cm) cake

This strawberry sponge cake is incredibly popular at Cakeboi. Customers are instantly transported to cloud nine as they bite into the light and airy cake crowned in pastel pink. The thing that sets this recipe apart from others is the luscious fresh fruit and a hint of rose water in the jam. You can taste the goodness of real strawberry flavor. This sponge is what summer is made of.

Strawberry and Rose Jam

3½ cups (500 g) strawberries, fresh or frozen

1⅔ cups (375 g) caster sugar

Juice of 1 lemon

1 tsp rose water

1 serving Versatile Vanilla Sponge Cake (page 63)

7 oz (200 ml) thickened or whipping cream

Strawberry Glaze

1⅛ cups (160 g) icing sugar

2 tsp (10 g) butter, melted

1 tbsp (18 g) Strawberry and Rose Jam (above)

1 tsp boiling water

½ pint (1 punnet) fresh strawberries, cut into quarters

Note: This is enough jam for your cake plus an additional jar to store in your fridge or to give to your neighbor.

Start this cake off the day before by making the Strawberry and Rose Jam.

Firstly, place a small plate in the freezer. Now, slice all the strawberries in half, then toss them in the sugar. Place the sugared strawberries in a large pot, add the lemon juice and rose water, then place it over a medium heat until it starts to simmer. Turn the heat down so that the jam does not reach a boil. Let it simmer for 10 minutes.

To test if the jam has reached the setting point, take a small spoonful of the hot jam, dollop it onto the frozen plate, and return the plate to the freezer for 1 minute. Take out the plate and run your finger through the jam. If the finger mark remains, the jam is set. Transfer the jam to a jar or container and let it set overnight.

The following day, prepare your Versatile Vanilla Sponge Cake as per page 63.

Now make the whipped cream. Pour the cream into a bowl and whisk it with an electric mixer fitted with a whisk attachment until firm peaks form.

For the glaze, place the sugar, melted butter, jam and boiling water in a heatproof bowl and mix until there are no lumps remaining. If the mixture is too thick, microwave it for 10 seconds to soften the glaze.

Assemble this cake as two separate layers before stacking them. For the bottom layer, place the cake on the cake stand, then dollop the whipped cream over the surface, followed by 1 tablespoon (15 ml) of the Strawberry and Rose Jam. Next, place the other layer of the cake on the counter and spread the glaze over the top. Do this before placing this cake layer on top of the bottom layer. Finally, arrange the quartered strawberries around the outside of the glaze to finish.

Raspberry Jam
Swiss Roll with Vanilla
Mascarpone Cream

Makes 1 Swiss roll

1 serving Versatile Vanilla
Sponge Cake (page 63)

Vanilla Mascarpone Cream

1 cup (250 g) mascarpone

½ cup (120 ml) thickened cream
or heavy cream

2 tbsp (20 g) icing sugar

1 tsp vanilla extract

¼ cup (80 g) raspberry jam
(page 30)

½ cup (70 g) icing sugar, for
dusting

This cake screams childhood to me. I remember taking store-bought Swiss rolls (or jam rolls, as they are also known) to school every day for recess. They were so delicious, the taste of the soft sponge with the sweet jam filling still remains in my memory. This recipe is something we have perfected at Cakeboi. The rolling does take some time to master, but be persistent; it is a handy skill to acquire. This cake is traditionally made with raspberries, but feel free to be creative and use coffee cream, strawberries, mango, pandan—the options are endless.

Firstly, you will need to prepare your Versatile Vanilla Sponge batter as per page 63, but you will be baking it a little differently. Instead of a round tin, prepare a baking tray about 12 x16 inches (30 x 40 cm) by placing baking paper flat on the bottom of the tray; do not grease the sides. Scrape the batter into the baking tray and smooth it into an even layer. Firmly tap the pan on the surface once, to remove any large air bubbles. Bake the cake until it's golden brown, firm and springy to the touch across the entire surface; this should take 12 to 15 minutes. Remove the sponge from the oven and leave it to cool slightly in the tray.

Whilst the cake is still slightly warm, dust a clean tea cloth with icing sugar. Turn your cake out onto the cloth. Peel away the baking paper, then carefully roll the sponge from one long side to the other long side with the cloth spiraled through the roll. Leave the sponge wrapped in the cloth until you're ready to decorate it.

To make the mascarpone cream filling, place the mascarpone, cream, sugar and vanilla in a medium-sized bowl. Using an electric mixer, whisk the mixture on high to form firm peaks.

Unroll your sponge and evenly spread your jam over the surface, leaving 1 inch (2.5 cm) at the side where the roll will end. Now spread the mascarpone cream over the jam, then using the tea cloth to guide it, roll the cake back up to enclose the filling.

Place the roll in the refrigerator for 30 minutes to allow the cream to set, then remove the tea cloth and trim both ends before dusting the roll in icing sugar.

Raspberry Jam Lamingtons

Makes 12 lamingtons

1 serving Versatile Vanilla Sponge Cake (page 63)

1 serving raspberry jam (page 30)

Chocolate Dip

7 cups (960 g) icing sugar

1 cup (100 g) cocoa powder

¼ cup (60 g) butter, melted

1½ cups (360 ml) boiling water

4½ cups (425 g) finely shredded coconut or desiccated coconut

The first time I went on MasterChef in 2018, I made a mousse-style dessert dedicated to my nan's lamingtons—think of it as a deconstructed lamington. That day, my dessert was named the top dish, which created some buzz about me and my nan's lamington recipe. I have to admit, I have not always been able to make a lamington. Since then, I have practiced making this cake and—oh my gosh, it is so much fun!

First, you will need to prepare your Versatile Vanilla Sponge batter as per page 63. However, you will be baking it a bit differently. Instead of a round tin, prepare a lamington tray measuring about 8 x 12 inches (20 x 30 cm) and more than 1 inch (at least 2.5 cm) high, by placing baking paper flat on the bottom of the tray; do not grease the sides. Scrape the batter into the lamington tray and smooth it into an even layer. Firmly tap the pan on the surface once to remove any large air bubbles. Bake the cake until it's golden brown, firm and springy to the touch across the entire surface, which should take 25 to 30 minutes. Remove the cake from the oven and leave it to cool in the tray.

Once the sponge is cooled completely, use a serrated knife to cut the sponge in half horizontally, creating two slabs. Spread the jam over one layer of the sponge, then place the second layer on top of the jam. Cut this sponge sandwich into thirds the long way, then into quarters by criss-crossing the first cuts, to form 12 squarish portions.

To make the chocolate dip, place the sugar, cocoa powder, melted butter and boiling water in a microwave-safe bowl and microwave it for 30 seconds, or until all the ingredients are well melted. Whisk to combine everything. This will create the glistening chocolate dip.

Now the fun part. Place a sheet of baking paper under a wire rack to act as a drip catcher for the excess chocolate. Place finely shredded coconut in a bowl next to your bowl of chocolate dip. Dip each piece of sponge sandwich into the chocolate, ensuring that it is fully coated, then toss it in the coconut. Place the laminton on a wire rack to set. Repeat this process until all twelve lamingtons are coated.

Nan's Passionfruit Custard Sponge Cake

Makes one 8-inch (20-cm) cake

Passionfruit Butter

4 egg yolks

¼ cup (60 g) caster sugar

⅓ cup (65 g) passionfruit pulp

⅓ cup (80 g) cold butter, cubed

Pinch of citric acid

This recipe is sentimental to me; it represents everything about my nan. This was Nan's signature cake. When I was growing up, it was one of my favorite cakes, and because of this Nan made it for my thirtieth birthday.

During my time on MasterChef, I practiced this cake nonstop. I didn't realize we were making memories at the time, but I would constantly call Nan to consult her, and she would coach, critique and guide me to perfecting it. I baked this cake on the show in tribute to her, and it brought Jock Zonfrillo to tears.

On the very last day of filming MasterChef, Nan passed away. Her memory still inspires me to this day. Cakeboi is a tribute to this incredible woman and mentor. I may no longer see you or talk to you, Nan, but you will live forever in my heart and mind. You are the most valued partner of Cakeboi. Your passionfruit custard cake is now a regular at Cakeboi, and it is one of the most popular cakes, too.

Your words and wisdom can now guide others . . .

Make the passionfruit butter one day prior to baking this cake, which is best served after setting in the fridge overnight. Bring the passionfruit butter together by combining the egg yolks, sugar and passionfruit pulp in a heatproof bowl and placing it over a pot of simmering water. Continually whisk the mixture until it lightens in color and thickens; it should resemble a hollandaise sauce. This may take up to 15 minutes, depending on the heat. You can test the consistency by lifting the whisk out of the mixture and drawing a number 8 with the dripping curd. If you're able to form the complete number 8 and it holds by the time you're finished, then the mixture is done.

Remove the bowl from the heat, then whisk in the cubed cold butter, one cube at a time. Add the citric acid and mix it in. Now transfer the passionfruit butter to a jar and place it in the fridge overnight.

(continued)

Nan's Passionfruit Custard Sponge Cake (Continued)

Custard Sponge

4 eggs

¾ cup (170 g) caster sugar

½ cup (75 g) custard powder

½ cup + 1½ tbsp (75 g) cornstarch

1 tsp cream of tartar

½ tsp baking soda

Passionfruit Icing

1½ cups (195 g) icing sugar, sifted

4 tsp (20 g) butter, melted

2 tbsp (25 g) passionfruit pulp

Orange and Vanilla Whipped Chantilly Cream

1 cup (240 ml) thickened or whipping cream

½ cup (70 g) icing sugar

Zest of 1 orange

1 tsp vanilla extract

For the sponge cake, start by preheating the oven to 355°F (180°C) fan forced, or, for a non-convection oven, 385°F (195°C). Line two 8-inch (20-cm) cake tins with baking paper. Begin the cake by placing the eggs and sugar in a bowl and beating them on high with an electric mixer for 10 minutes. *Nan was always very specific about beating the eggs for exactly 10 minutes.*

Whilst the eggs are beating, prepare the dry ingredients by sifting the custard powder, cornstarch, cream of tartar and soda onto a sheet of baking paper. Transfer the sifted ingredients back into a bowl, then sift them back onto the baking paper again. Repeat this process two more times. *Nan was very specific about the number of times that they needed to be sifted.*

Using a large spoon, carefully start to fold the dry ingredients into the egg mixture. Gently continue to fold until all the dry ingredients are well incorporated and the custard powder colors the batter.

Divide the batter between the two cake tins, then place them in the oven for 25 minutes. Allow the baked sponge layers to cool before removing them from the tins. You may need to run a knife around the inside of the tin to release the sponge.

For the passionfruit icing, mix together the icing sugar, melted butter and passionfruit pulp.

For the Chantilly cream, place the cream, icing sugar, orange zest and vanilla in a bowl and whisk on high for about 1 minute, or until you have firm peaks. Be careful not to over-whisk and split the cream.

To assemble the cake, place one layer on a cake stand and dollop the Chantilly cream over it. Spoon the set passionfruit butter over the top of the cream, then place the top layer of the sponge on this bottom layer. Finally, pour the passionfruit icing over the top of the cake, covering the whole layer.

Elva's Blow-Away Chocolate Sponge with Whipped Cream, Ganache and Raspberry Jam

Makes one 8-inch (20-cm) cake

Chocolate Sponge Cake

6 eggs

¾ cup (170 g) sugar

¾ cup (105 g) cornstarch

½ cup (60 g) self-rising flour

4 tbsp (25 g) cocoa powder

1 tsp cream of tartar

I've always enjoyed tennis; I was born into it. Nan played social tennis every week, and my brothers and I would accompany her from a young age. As time progressed, so too did our tennis skills. We would often hit a ball against the clubhouse wall, mimicking Nan on the court.

In 2018, I joined a local small tennis club run by a lovely lady named Elva. This club advocated for me during my time on MasterChef. I'd often find my articles pinned to their notice board. I noticed a lot of similarities between Elva and my nan—both loved tennis and baking. Elva and I would banter about baking, and she once served me this sponge recipe. Beware of a slight breeze; it is so light and delicate, a tennis ball might not be the only thing gliding by. With this blow-away sponge, the crowd will be in a frenzy.

Game, set, match!

For the sponge cake, preheat the oven to 355°F (180°C) fan forced, or, for a non-convection oven, 385°F (195°C). Prepare two 8-inch (20-cm) baking tins, cutting baking paper into a round shape the size of the tin. Place the baking paper in the bottom of the tin, but do not grease the sides. With a sponge, I prefer not to grease the sides, so that the sponge can cling to the tin, allowing for a better rise.

With an electric mixer on a high speed, beat the eggs and the sugar until thick, light and foamy. This may take 10 minutes. Then sift together the cornstarch, self-rising flour, cocoa powder and cream of tartar—Elva's secret is to sift all the dry ingredients to ensure the lightest batter possible—and fold these dry ingredients into the beaten eggs.

(continued)

Elva's Blow-Away Chocolate Sponge with Whipped Cream, Ganache and Raspberry Jam (Continued)

Chocolate Ganache

4 oz (125 g) bittersweet (50–60%) chocolate

1 cup (240 ml) thickened or whipping cream

Whipped Chantilly Cream

1 cup (240 ml) thickened cream or whipping cream

½ cup (70 g) icing sugar

1 tsp vanilla extract

3 tbsp (50 g) raspberry jam (page 30)

Divide this mixture between the two tins and bake them for 26 minutes. Once they are cooked, run a butter knife around the outside of each sponge to release it from the tin. Rest and cool the cakes on a rack.

For the ganache, chop the chocolate until it is in small cubes of about ¼ inch (6 mm), then place them in a heatproof bowl.

Pour the cream into a small saucepan and place it on the stove over a low heat. Gently heat the cream until it starts to simmer. As the small simmering bubbles appear, remove the cream from the heat and pour it over the chocolate.

Stir the cream and chocolate until the chocolate is melted and has formed into a ganache. Set this to the side in the fridge to cool until it is the consistency of mayonnaise.

For the Chantilly cream, place the cream, icing sugar and vanilla in a bowl and whisk them on high until you have firm peaks.

To assemble the cake, place the first layer of the sponge on the cake stand. Dollop the Chantilly cream onto the bottom layer of the cake, followed by the raspberry jam. Add the top layer of sponge, then drizzle the chocolate ganache over the sponge, covering the whole top layer. Allow the ganache to drip over the sides to create a beautiful homey effect.

Ginger Fluff Sponge with Caramelized Condensed Milk Chantilly Cream

Makes one 8-inch (20-cm) cake

1 tbsp (14 g) butter

1 tbsp (15 ml) golden syrup

4 eggs, separated

¾ cup (170 g) caster sugar

½ cup + 1½ tbsp (75 g) cornstarch

4 tbsp (30 g) all-purpose flour

1 tsp cocoa powder

1 tsp ground cinnamon

1½ tsp (6 g) ground ginger

Caramelized Condensed Milk Chantilly Cream

7 oz (195 g) caramelized condensed milk (page 14), chilled

½ cup (120 ml) thickened or whipping cream

1 tsp cocoa powder, for dusting

Tips and Tricks: Outside of Australia and the UK, you may not be familiar with golden syrup. It is a toffee-flavored syrup with the consistency of honey. The best substitute for golden syrup is one part molasses or treacle and three parts honey—the flavor is nearly identical.

This is another recipe from Nan's handwritten cookbook. She named it a ginger cake, but after researching it further, I realized it is a ginger fluff sponge. This Australian classic is absolutely beautiful; it is light as air, with a gorgeous spiced cocoa flavor. It has a generous amount of golden syrup and cream. This cake is as divine as it sounds. I tweaked Nan's recipe by adding caramelized condensed milk and Chantilly cream. I believe caramel and spice make things oh-so-nice. This cake is a lighter, fluffier gingerbread, oozing with cream.

Preheat the oven to 355°F (180°C) fan forced, or, for a non-convection oven, 385°F (195°C). Prepare an 8-inch (20-cm) baking tin, cutting baking paper into a round shape the size of the tin. Place the baking paper in the bottom of the tin, but do not grease the sides. With a sponge, I prefer not to grease the sides, so that the sponge can cling to the tin, allowing for a better rise.

Place the butter and golden syrup in a microwave-safe bowl and heat for 30 seconds to melt the butter. Now place it on the counter so it comes to room temperature. Using an electric mixer with a whisk attachment, beat the egg whites on high until they start to foam. Gradually add the caster sugar, one spoon at a time, then beat until the egg whites are at a stiff peak. Fold them through the egg yolks.

Meanwhile, as time allows, sift the cornstarch, flour, cocoa powder, cinnamon and ginger into a bowl, then repeat this process four times to ensure a super light mixture. Once they are sifted, fold the dry ingredients into the whipped eggs as carefully as you can, trying not to overwork the mixture. Now fold in the butter and the golden syrup.

Pour the batter into the tin, then place it on the middle rack of the oven. Bake it for 18 to 20 minutes, or until the sponge is set through. Only ever check the sponge after 18 minutes. Turn it out onto a wire rack to cool.

For the Chantilly cream, place the chilled caramelized condensed milk and the cream in a bowl and, using an electric mixer, whisk until soft peaks form.

To assemble the cake, slice it horizontally into two layers. Place the bottom layer on your cake stand, dollop all of the cream onto this layer, and spread it out to cover. Add the final layer of cake, then generously dust the cake with the remaining cocoa powder.

Makes one 8-inch (20-cm) cake

Airy, bouncy, light and sweet, this is a recipe for a soft, tender and fluffy sponge cake that's bursting with citrus flavor from the fresh orange juice and zest used. Now, don't be afraid to experiment. Seasonal citruses can all rotate through this cake—regular oranges, blood oranges, mandarines, kumquats, even a beautiful Meyer lemon.

Vanilla Diplomat Cream

1 serving Pastry Cream (page 37)

½ cup (120 ml) whipping cream

Orange Sponge

¾ cup (180 g) butter

2 tsp (4 g) orange zest

3 oz (90 ml) orange juice

1 cup (240 ml) water

6 eggs

1¼ cups (280 g) caster sugar

2½ cups (315 g) self-rising flour

Poached Blood Orange Segments

1 cup (200 g) sugar

1 cup (240 ml) water

1 vanilla bean

2 blood oranges, segmented

Blood Orange Vanilla Icing

1 cup (140 g) icing sugar

Juice of ½ small blood orange

The best place to start is with the vanilla diplomat cream. This will need to be made at least 5 hours before decorating the cake. Prepare the pastry cream as per page 37. Once it is cooled, whisk it together with the whipping cream, firstly to loosen the set custard, then until there are no lumps remaining and soft peaks are formed. Place it in the fridge until needed.

For the sponge cake, preheat the oven to 355°F (180°C) fan forced, or, for a non-convection oven, 385°F (195°C). Prepare two 8-inch (20-cm) baking tins, cutting baking paper into a round shape to cover the bottom of the tins. Now line the sides of the tins with extra baking paper, which will sit above the lip of the tin. This will help the sponge in case it rises above the lip.

Place the butter, orange zest, orange juice and water in a small saucepan and heat it to melt the butter. Put it to the side to cool. In a stand mixer with a whisk attachment, beat the eggs and the sugar together on a medium-high speed for 12 minutes. Sift the flour into the aerated eggs and fold it through until no lumps are remaining, then carefully fold through the cooled butter mixture.

Divide the batter between the two tins and place them on the middle rack of the oven. Bake for 22 minutes, or until the sponge is set through. Remove the tins from the oven and let them sit for 2 minutes, then carefully turn the cake layers out onto a wire rack that is covered with a clean tea towel (this sponge can be sticky).

For the poached orange segments, bring the sugar, water and vanilla bean to a boil. Place the orange segments in a heatproof bowl and pour the hot syrup over them. After 10 minutes, remove the segments from the syrup and allow them to cool.

To make the orange icing, mix the icing sugar with the orange juice in a bowl until smooth.

To assemble the cake, place the bottom layer on your cake stand. Dollop the diplomat cream onto this layer of cake and spread it to cover the top. Add half of the orange segments, followed by the final layer of cake. Drizzle the orange icing over the top of the cake. Smooth it out with the back of a spoon. Decorate the cake with the remaining blood orange segments.

Orange Sponge
with Vanilla
Diplomat Cream

Chiffon Sponge Cake

Makes one 9-inch (23-cm) cake

1⅔ cups (200 g) all-purpose flour, or cake flour if possible for softest result

2 tsp (10 g) baking powder

½ cup (120 ml) vegetable oil

⅔ cup (160 ml) milk

1 tbsp (15 ml) vanilla extract

7 eggs, separated

1 tsp lemon juice

½ cup (110 g) caster sugar

Chiffon cake (pronounced SHE-fon) is prized for its very light, pillowy soft and cottony texture that just melts in your mouth.

Chiffon cake has a high ratio of eggs to flour and becomes light as air because so much air is beaten into the egg whites. It's similar to an angel food cake and sort of like a sponge cake, but instead of using just egg whites, chiffon cake recipes use the whole egg, and unlike a sponge, this cake has oil added to the batter. Adding these extra ingredients gives the cake a silky moist texture and a richer, more flavorful taste.

When baking this cake, I always would use an uncoated two-piece chiffon tin, never a nonstick tin. This tin is important, as it will encourage the cake to climb up the sides, resulting in a better rise. Like most sponges that I make, I never grease the tin.

Preheat your oven to 340°F (170°C) fan forced, or, for a non-convection oven, 365°F (185°C). For this cake, I always use a 9-inch (23-cm) chiffon cake tin. This tin is designed to easily remove the cake. Just run a knife around the sides and pop the bottom out. Carefully ease the cake from the base.

To start this cake, sift your flour and baking powder together. The general rule for this cake is to sift the flour three times. In a medium mixing bowl, whisk together your vegetable oil, milk, vanilla and egg yolks. Now gradually add your flour whilst whisking to form a smooth paste.

In a large bowl, place in your egg whites and the lemon juice. Now, with an electric mixer fitted with a whisk attachment, whisk the eggs on a medium speed until they become light and fluffy, approximately 1 to 2 minutes. With the mixer still running, start to feed the sugar in, one tablespoon at a time, until all the sugar is mixed with the eggs. Continue to whisk the egg whites until they form stiff peaks. This meringue should take about 8 to 10 minutes.

(continued)

Chiffon Sponge Cake (Continued)

Berry, Lemon and Yogurt Icing

¾ cup (180 g) Greek yogurt

1 tsp vanilla extract

1 tbsp (18 g) Basic Berry Jam (page 30)

½ cup (70 g) icing sugar

With a spatula, fold one-third of the meringue through the egg yolk paste to create a more workable batter. Next, fold the remaining meringue through the batter, ensuring that no white streaks of meringue remain.

Pour the batter into the tin, then insert a skewer and run it around the center of the cake; this will help eliminate any air bubbles. Firmly tap the cake once before placing it in the oven to cook for 50 to 55 minutes. To test this cake, gently press on the surface, and if it's light and springy, then it is ready to be cooled.

When you remove the cake from the oven, place the tin upside-down on a cooling rack to help it stretch downwards instead of collapsing. Leave it upside-down for at least 6 hours before removing the cake from the tin.

For the icing, simply mix the yogurt, vanilla, jam and sugar together.

When assembling this cake, carefully run a knife around the sides of the tin to release the cake, then repeat on the bottom of the tin. The base of this cake will serve as the top presentation side. Dollop the icing over the cake and allow it to drizzle down the sides.

Powder Puffs with Mascarpone and White Chocolate

Makes 6

3 eggs, separated

½ cup (110 g) caster sugar

½ tsp vanilla extract

½ cup (60 g) all-purpose flour

4 tsp (10 g) cornstarch

½ tsp baking powder

Powder puffs are sometimes known as sponge kisses or sponge drops. Regardless of what you call them, they are soft, light, fluffy and absolutely delicious. These cakes supposedly got their name from their resemblance to the powder puffs that are used to dust makeup upon one's face. Luckily, they taste much better than their namesake! Powder puffs were something my great-nan Groves would make all the time, and they were a favorite of my mother's.

Powder puffs are airy, soft mini sponge cakes, paired with a generous amount of fresh cream between them. They are at their best if made the day before, or at least refrigerated for 6 hours before serving. This will allow the puffs to soften up.

Preheat the oven to 375°F (190°C) fan forced, or, for a non-convection oven, 400°F (205°C). Line two baking trays with baking paper.

This recipe uses the same ingredients—eggs, caster sugar, vanilla, flour, cornstarch and baking powder—as the Versatile Vanilla Sponge Cake, with half the amounts. Follow the method on page 63; however, I would recommend just using a handheld electric mixer over a stand mixer. The smaller batter size might not aerate in a large mixer.

To shape the powder puffs, place either a 2½-inch (6-cm) ring cutter or an egg ring on the baking tray, then spoon in the sponge batter until it covers the whole surface. Repeat this process until all the batter is used up.

Place the trays in the oven and bake for 10 to 12 minutes, or until the centers of individual cakes bounce back. Turn the cakes out onto a wire rack to cool.

(continued)

Powder Puffs with Mascarpone and White Chocolate (Continued)

White Chocolate and Mascarpone Icing

7 oz (200 g) white chocolate, chopped fine

¾ cup (180 ml) whipping cream

1 cup (250 g) mascarpone

1⅛ cups (250 g) butter, at room temperature

1 tbsp (15 ml) vanilla extract

1 cup (140 g) icing sugar

2 tbsp (20 g) icing sugar, for dusting

For the icing, place the white chocolate and cream in a large heatproof bowl over a pot of simmering water. Carefully heat until all the lumps of chocolate are melted, then remove the bowl from the heat and place it in the fridge to cool for 15 minutes, or until it is no longer warm.

In a large mixing bowl, with an electric mixer fitted with a paddle attachment, beat the mascarpone, butter and vanilla until light and fluffy. Add the cooled white chocolate on a low speed, and beat to incorporate. Add the icing sugar, then beat once again to create a smooth, light icing.

To assemble the cakes, drop dollops of icing from a dessert spoon onto the flat side of one of the puffs, then top with a second, sandwiching them together. Repeat until all the puffs are filled. Dust with icing sugar.

4.
Premier Pastries

If cooking is considered an art form, a great artist is one who has mastered the technique of making pastry. I owe my skills to Newcastle's renowned and remarkable French chef, Lesley Taylor. She is a delightful and dedicated chef who is particular and precise in her practice and presentation. Lesley helped me perfect my artistry whilst we worked together.

Only a few ingredients are needed to make all types of pastry—flour, fat, salt and water. I like to think of pastry as a versatile medium that is basically just delicious "edible packaging." I have always had a fascination with and love for pastry. I find it a relaxing practice. Rolling dough is soothing, and it calms me. This might seem strange, as some deem pastry too time-consuming, and others too complicated or strenuous. This doesn't have to be the case. I would recommend trying the Raspberry Almond Frangipane Tart (page 91) or the Toasty Caramel Meringue Tart (page 94) before moving onto something like My Signature Lemon Tart (page 97) or the Chocolate Custard Tart with Caramelized Condensed Milk (page 92). Just ensure you read each of the following recipes carefully; the tips and tricks are mentioned for a reason. I find the biggest mistake one can make is not packing the beads firmly enough when blind baking.

Once you have learnt the techniques and secrets of good pastry making, you too might find pastry relaxing. So roll away the stresses of the day with some Zen baking, then sit back and enjoy the tasty treats you have created.

Raspberry and Vanilla Cream Puffs

Makes 16 cream puffs

Craquelin

6 tbsp (90 g) butter

6 tbsp (90 g) raw sugar

¾ cup (90 g) all-purpose flour

Choux Pastry

7 tbsp (100 g) butter

1 scant cup (225 ml) water

1 tsp salt

1 tsp caster sugar

1½ cups (180 g) all-purpose flour

4 eggs plus 1 yolk

1 tsp vanilla extract

This iconic dessert is made with a French pastry known as choux pastry (pronounced "shoo"). It is also known as pâte à choux. Nan would refer to choux pastry as profiteroles or cream puffs. At Cakeboi we add a layer of craquelin on top of the pastry dough. This encourages the choux to cook evenly as it puffs up, giving a beautiful round surface.

Choux has a reputation for being difficult, but I've learnt a new method, and it's surprisingly simple. This recipe was taught to me by the choux queen, MasterChef 2020 winner Emilia Jackson. Traditionally, I would always make my choux pastry with milk until Emilia showed me this method. Replacing milk with water produces steam that helps create a better hollow center in a lighter puff.

To make the craquelin, place the butter, raw sugar and flour in a bowl and mix to create a paste. Place the paste between two sheets of baking paper, then roll it to approximately ⅛ inch (3 mm) thick. Move the craquelin to the freezer until needed. This will firm up the butter and make it much easier to handle.

For the choux pastry, preheat the oven to 320°F (160°C) and prepare a baking tray with baking paper. Place the butter, water, salt and caster sugar in a medium-sized saucepan and set it over a medium-high heat. Bring it to a boil, remove it from the heat, then add the flour and stir vigorously until no lumps remain. Return to a medium heat, continually stirring the dough for 3 to 5 minutes, or until a crust forms at the base of the pan.

Transfer the dough to a stand mixer with a paddle attachment (an electric handheld mixer or a hand whisk is also sufficient). On a low speed, beat the mixture to release all of the steam. Once the steam has dissipated, with the mixer running, add the eggs one at a time, followed by the vanilla. Transfer the dough to a piping bag.

Remove the craquelin from the freezer, then use a ring cutter to cut 1¼-inch (3-cm) disks. (If you do not have a ring cutter, you can always use a narrow glass such as a champagne flute.) Now pipe out the choux pastry dough onto the baking tray to create 1¼-inch (3-cm) domes, ensuring that they are spaced well apart, then top each with a craquelin disk.

1 serving Pastry Cream (page 37)

1 serving raspberry Basic Berry Jam (page 30)

Splash a small amount of water over the pastry, then place it in the preheated oven. Do not open the oven door for the first 30 minutes. Bake for 30 to 45 minutes, or until the pastry is evenly caramelized. Check the choux by cutting a small hole in the bottom of one to see if there is any raw pastry remaining; if so, return them to the oven for an additional 5 minutes.

Make the pastry cream as per page 37.

Make the jam as per page 30.

To assemble the cream puffs, transfer the pastry cream into one piping bag and some raspberry jam into a second piping bag. Using a chopstick, punch a hole into the base of each puff. Now pipe a small amount of raspberry jam into the cavity, then fill the remaining space with the vanilla cream. Continue until all puffs are filled.

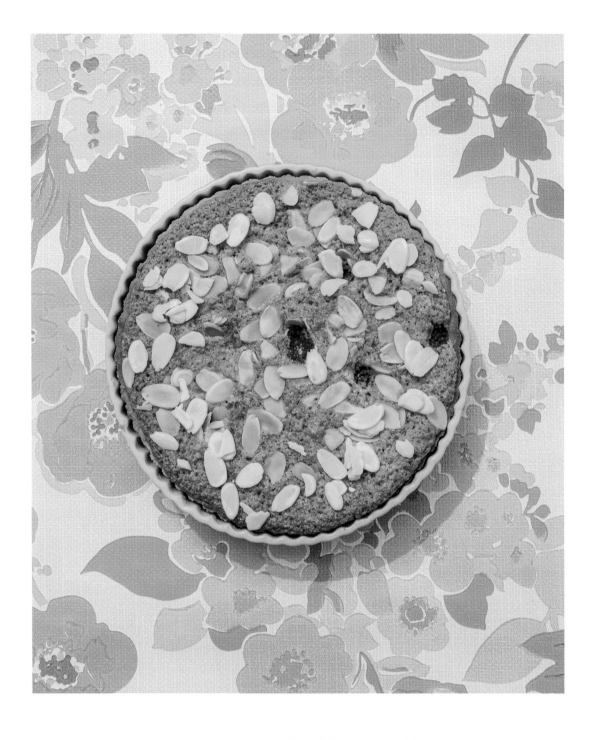

Raspberry Almond Frangipane Tart

Makes one 10-inch (25-cm) tart

Like a siren, this French tart lures customers towards the Cakeboi display cabinet, singing sweet-bitter songs, fooling them with its simplistic and humble outward appearance. But once it is cut, people are mesmerized by the speckled raspberry diamonds woven within its core. The struggle is real, and you can't resist the temptation.

This tart is not too sweet, not too crumbly, but just right—the perfect balance. I achieved this through experimenting and tweaking countless recipes until I mastered what I believe is the perfect raspberry almond frangipane tart.

Jouer sur le velours!

Frangipane Filling

½ cup + 1 tbsp (120 g) brown sugar

½ cup (110 g) caster sugar

1 scant cup (200 g) butter, at room temperature

4 eggs, at room temperature

1 scant cup (90 g) almond meal

¾ cup (100 g) self-rising flour

Pinch of salt

1 serving raspberry Basic Berry Jam (page 30)

1 serving Go-To Sweet Pastry Crust (page 18), blind baked

¼ cup (25 g) sliced almonds

½ cup (64 g) raspberries, fresh or frozen

Firstly, preheat the oven to 280°F (140°C).

For the frangipane filling, place both sugars and the butter in a large mixing bowl. Using an electric mixer, beat the butter for about 3 to 4 minutes, or until it is light and fluffy. Turn the mixer down to low, then add the eggs one at a time. Do not add the next egg until the previous egg is fully mixed through. From time to time you may need to scrape down the sides of the bowl.

Once the eggs are thoroughly mixed in, turn off the mixer and sift the almond meal, self-rising flour and salt into the mixture. Then, using a spatula, carefully fold the flour through, ensuring that you do not deflate the batter.

To assemble the tart, put 3 tablespoons of the jam in the blind-baked pastry shell and spread it to cover the base. Fill the tart shell with the frangipane filling and spread it into an even layer. Scatter the sliced almonds over the surface of the tart, then repeat with the raspberries.

Place the tart in the oven and bake it for 55 to 60 minutes, until the frangipane mixture rises over the edges of the tart shell and is golden in color. Cool it completely before slicing.

Chocolate Custard Tart with Caramelized Condensed Milk

Makes one 10-inch (25-cm) tart

7 oz (195 g) caramelized condensed milk (page 14)

1 serving Chocolate Pastry Crust (page 25), blind baked

Custard Filling

9 egg yolks

⅓ cup (75 g) raw sugar

2 cups (480 ml) thickened cream or heavy cream

7 oz (200 g) bittersweet (around 54%) chocolate, chopped into fine pieces

This heavenly chocolate tart is well worth the effort. Caramelized condensed milk, also known as dulce de leche, goes beautifully with the baked bitter chocolate filling. There is a refined elegance about dulce de leche desserts. They look divine and taste delicious. Dulce de leche is a caramelized reduction of milk and sugar, whereas caramel is a reduction of butter and sugar.

This impressive tart is sweet, gooey, bitter and a little salty. It is a truly indulgent dessert. This recipe will leave you with some leftover egg whites; don't waste them. You can whip them into meringues for some extra treats.

There are a couple of steps to be done the day prior for this recipe. First, you will need to make your caramelized condensed milk, following the directions on page 14, and place the can in the fridge overnight to set. (Alternatively, dulce de leche is becoming increasingly popular in the supermarkets.)

Also, prepare your pastry as per page 25. Leave the blind-baked tart shell in its baking tin.

The next day, position a rack in the middle of the oven and preheat to 265°F (130°C). To begin the custard filling, place the egg yolks and sugar in a bowl, then whisk until they begin to lighten in color. Place the cream in a small saucepan over medium heat and bring it to a simmer. Pour one-third of the heated cream onto the eggs, then quickly whisk it through. Add the remaining cream, whisk again, then add the chocolate. The chocolate will melt from the heat in the cream. Cool the custard in the fridge until it thickens.

To fill the tart, give the dulce de leche a quick stir in the tin. This will loosen it for easier spreading. Spoon the dulce de leche over the base of the tart shell. Set the tart shell in its tin on a baking tray and place it in the oven. Pour the custard filling into the shell, then gently close the oven door.

Bake for 45 to 50 minutes, or until the custard is set with a very slight jiggle. Set the tart in the refrigerator until fully cooled before slicing.

Makes one 10-inch (25-cm) tart

1 serving Go-To Sweet Pastry Crust (page 18), blind baked

Caramel Filling

1 cup + 2 tsp (250 ml) milk

1 cup (200 g) brown sugar

2 tbsp (15 g) all-purpose flour

3 egg yolks

1 tsp vanilla extract

¼ tsp salt

1 tbsp (14 g) butter

Meringue

3 egg whites

¾ cup (170 g) caster sugar

⅛ tsp cream of tartar

Tips and Tricks: You can do the torching right after spreading the meringue, and then place the tart in the fridge for an hour, or until needed. This will help keep the meringue intact. But if you are serving the tart to guests seated around your dining table, deploying your blowtorch in front of them is an undeniably impressive spectacle.

This tart came to life at Cakeboi during the COVID-19 lockdown. We attempted so many things to try to keep our business alive. Some worked, and others did not. One saving grace was creating high tea boxes for pickup and delivery. The idea was a hit, and during this tough time we were able to keep things afloat because of them.

Nan would serve this tart when we went to her house for our weekly barbecues, and it was something we all looked forward to. To finish the tart, Nan would toast the meringue in the oven. However, at Cakeboi we use a blowtorch (which I call the flamethrower). It creates the same effect, but I like to live dangerously.

Firstly, prepare your pastry as per page 18.

To start the caramel filling, pour your milk into a small saucepan and bring it to a simmer. In a large heatproof bowl, whisk together the brown sugar, flour and egg yolks; this mixture will be quite thick. Once the milk has come to a simmer, pour one-third of it onto the egg and sugar mixture, then quickly whisk it through. Add the remaining milk and the vanilla and salt, and whisk to combine it all.

In a saucepan that will be large enough to fit the base of your heatproof bowl, bring some water to a boil over a high heat. Place your bowl over the boiling water to create a bain-marie and continually stir it with a whisk. Cook the mixture until it thickens to the consistency of heavy cream. This may take up to 10 minutes.

Once it has thickened, add the butter then whisk until smooth. Pour the mixture into the prepared tart shell then place it to the side.

To make the meringue, with an electric mixer, whip the egg whites until they start to foam. Mix together the caster sugar and cream of tartar, then add this to the egg whites one spoon at a time. Continue until all the sugar is added and the meringue reaches a stiff peak. (This can be tested by lifting the whisk out of the meringue; if the peak stands vertically, then it is ready.) Spread the meringue over the tart. Chill the tart for at least an hour, or until just before serving.

Now it's time to torch. If you have a blowtorch, brown the meringue with the flame, being careful not to leave the flame on one spot for too long. If you do not have a blowtorch, then place the tart in a 320°F (160°C) preheated oven for 5 minutes to brown the top just prior to serving.

Toasty Caramel Meringue Tart

My Signature Lemon Tart

Makes one 8-inch (20-cm) tart

6 eggs

1⅛ cups (250 g) caster sugar

½ cup + 4 tsp (140 ml) lemon juice, from approximately 3 large lemons

1 tsp citric acid

1 serving Go-To Sweet Pastry Crust (page 18)

Firstly, if you nail this recipe on the first go, I take my hat off to you. However, don't let this comment deter you. When I look at my lemon tart, my reflection tells a story of my passion and career. This stellar tart built my business and now secured my book. This is my most requested recipe. I owe everything to this showstopping dessert.

I treasure this recipe. For so long, I've held it close to my chest, but now I share it with you . . .

This tart is a two-day project. It is best to make the filling for this tart one day prior to baking.

On the first day, make the filling. In a large bowl, whisk together the eggs, sugar, lemon juice and citric acid until no clumps of egg white remain. Now pass the mixture through a fine sieve to remove any unincorporated egg. Mixing the ingredients will agitate the eggs, causing them to aerate. Cover the mixture, then rest it in the fridge overnight. As the mixture sits overnight, the foam will slowly float to the surface, leaving a clear, glossy mixture underneath.

The following day, prepare your pastry as per page 18, and set the blind-baked shell aside to cool in its tin. Reduce the oven setting to 250°F (120°C), and position your rack at the middle level.

Remove the filling mixture from the fridge, then begin the skimming process. Using a ladle, carefully lift the foam off the surface. Once all the foam is removed, lay a paper towel on the surface, then lift to remove remaining air bubbles. I often repeat the skimming and the paper towel until there are no impurities left on the surface. This mixture is now ready to bake.

Place your prepared tart shell in its tin on a baking tray and set it in the oven. Carefully pour the lemon mixture into the tart shell until it reaches the top. Close the door gently, and bake for 30 minutes, then check every 5 minutes until you have a set tart. When checking to see if the lemon curd is set, you will need to gently wobble the tart. What you are looking for is an even wobble that looks like a wobbling unmolded jelly. Transfer the tart to the fridge and allow it to chill.

Makes one 10-inch (25-cm) tart

1 serving Go-To Sweet Pastry Crust (page 18) blind baked

Honey-Roasted Figs

8 fresh figs

1 vanilla bean

⅓ cup (80 ml) honey

Brown Butter Filling

½ cup (115 g) butter

2 eggs

⅔ cup (150 g) caster sugar

¼ cup (35 g) all-purpose flour

1 vanilla bean

1 tbsp (10 g) icing sugar

This tart comes with an amazing MasterChef story. This recipe is called the golden brown butter tart because it was a dish I cooked on MasterChef during a "golden mystery box challenge." This particular challenge pitted me against the dessert king Reynold. We were both cooking sweets on the same bench. Reynold is an absolute wizard of modern cooking; he is so intelligent with his ideas. The MasterChef team contrasted us by building up a story arc of a classic-versus-modern dessert-off. Spoiler alert, my classic humble brown butter tart placed me on the top.

Firstly, prepare your pastry as per page 18. This can be done the day before.

I would suggest that you also roast your figs the night before. This gives them enough time to sit in their own juices and soak up all the delicious vanilla. If you're pressed for time, though, this can be done only a few hours earlier.

Preheat your oven to 300°F (150°C). To start the roasted figs, cut them in half, then place them in a roasting tin. Cut the vanilla pod down the center lengthwise. With your knife at a 45-degree angle, run the knife down the cut side of the pod to release the seeds. Add the seeds, the pod and the honey to the figs, and toss to coat them. Cover the tray with foil, then place it in the oven for 15 to 20 minutes to soften the figs. Pour the figs and syrup into a container and store them in the refrigerator overnight.

The next day, preheat your oven to 300°F (150°C). It's time to start on the filling. Firstly, place your butter in a saucepan over medium heat until it melts and slowly comes to a boil. The butter will begin to foam; stir it constantly, as the milk solids will cling to the bottom of the pan. Cook the butter until the milk solids begin to caramelize and release a nutty aroma. Pour the butter into a bowl, then allow it to cool to room temperature.

Place your eggs and caster sugar in the bowl of an electric mixer and whisk them on a high speed until they are doubled in size, approximately 10 minutes. Sift in the flour and the seeds from the vanilla bean, removed from their pod the same way as earlier. Using a hand whisk, fold the mixture until it is evenly combined. Once the flour is incorporated, pour the brown butter into the bowl and, using the hand whisk, gently fold the butter into the mixture.

To assemble your tart, arrange your honey-roasted figs in the baked tart shell, then pour the filling over the figs. Place the tart in the oven and bake for 40 to 45 minutes; the top of the tart should be slightly golden. Cool the tart to room temperature, then dust it with icing sugar.

Golden Brown Butter Tart
with Honey-Roasted Figs

Peach and Rosé Tart

**Makes one 8-inch
(20-cm) tart**

This recipe is for all of the people who swoon over stunning pastries and believe wine is a staple. Peach and Rosé Tart is made with delicious sweet summer peaches, almond pastry and perfectly pink rosé. It is a match made in heaven. Not only is this tart pretty; it's a delicious flavor combo that's dressed to impress.

1 serving Almond Pastry Crust
(page 22)

Firstly, prepare your almond pastry as per page 22. To start the filling, pour your cream and milk into a medium saucepan. Take half of a vanilla pod that you have divided crosswise, and slit it vertically. Scrape out the seeds with a knife, add them to the saucepan, and then slowly bring it to a gentle simmer.

Pastry Cream

1¼ cups (300 ml) thickened or
whipping cream

7 oz (200 ml) milk

½ vanilla bean

⅓ cup (75 g) caster sugar

¼ cup (30 g) cornstarch

5 egg yolks

7 tbsp (100 g) butter, cold

In the meantime, place your caster sugar and cornstarch in a medium-sized heatproof bowl, then whisk them together to break up any clumps. Add the egg yolks, then quickly whisk the mixture together. It might start very lumpy, but it will smooth out.

Temper the eggs by adding a small amount of the hot cream whilst continually whisking. Add the cream little by little until half the cream is whisked through the eggs, bringing them to temperature. Transfer the warmed eggs to the saucepan, then bring it to a simmer. Stirring continually, cook the mixture until it becomes quite thick and reaches a boil.

Pour the cream into a bowl and then, whilst continually whisking, add the butter, about 1 tablespoon (14 g) at a time. Once it is fully incorporated, pour the pastry cream into the prepared tart shell. Now place a layer of cling wrap over the surface of the cream, then place the tart in the refrigerator for 1 hour to set.

Poaching Syrup

½ cup (100 g) sugar

1 cup (240 ml) rosé wine

½ vanilla bean

To make the syrup, place the sugar, the rosé wine and the seeds and pod of the remaining half a vanilla bean in a medium-sized saucepan, then bring the mixture to a boil. Stir to dissolve any remaining sugar.

4 white peaches

4 tbsp (30 g) flaked almonds
(optional)

Cut the white peaches into quarters and place them in the boiling syrup for 30 seconds, then turn the heat off. Leave the peaches in the hot syrup for 5 minutes, then remove them with a spoon. Return the syrup to a boil and reduce it by three-quarters. Now turn off the heat and cool the syrup completely.

Remove the cling wrap from the tart. Arrange the peaches over the set pastry cream. Lightly brush the peaches with the reduced syrup, then sprinkle the tart with flaked almonds (if using).

Smoky Bourbon and Vanilla Pecan Pie

Makes one 10-inch (25-cm) pie

1 serving Go-To Sweet Pastry (page 18)

2½ cups (240 g) pecan halves, divided

3 eggs

⅔ cup + 1 tbsp (155 g) light brown sugar

1 vanilla bean

⅓ cup (80 g) butter, melted

¾ cup (180 ml) maple syrup

2 tbsp (15 g) all-purpose flour

Pinch of salt

3 tbsp (45 ml) smoky bourbon

Boozy Custard

4 egg yolks

2 tbsp (15 g) cornstarch

2½ cups (600 ml) milk

3 tbsp (40 g) sugar

2 tbsp (30 ml) smoky bourbon

Reserved vanilla bean pod

Oh, it's been one of those weeks. Do you know what I mean? Do you feel like you need a little southern kick to get you through? Well, I have a treat for you!

If you think you can't love pecan pie any more than you already do, add bourbon. It makes such a delicious difference! The bourbon is bold, but not overwhelming. It enhances the other ingredients with a touch of its rich, smoky flavor, and it takes pecan pie to a heavenly place.

Prepare the Go-To Sweet Pastry as per page 18.

Preheat the oven to 355°F (180°C) fan forced, or, for a non-convection oven, 385°F (195°C).

To start the pie filling, spread half of the pecans on a baking tray, then place them in the oven for 5 minutes to roast. Allow the toasted pecans to cool before roughly chopping them. Reserve them on the side, and leave the remaining pecan halves intact. Reduce the oven to 320°F (160°C) fan forced, or, for a non-convection oven, 345°F (175°C).

In a large mixing bowl, whisk together your eggs and light brown sugar until smooth. Slit the vanilla bean lengthwise, then scrape the seeds out with the knife and add them to the bowl. (Reserve the vanilla pod for the custard.) Add the melted butter, maple syrup, flour, salt and bourbon, then whisk to combine. Stir in the chopped roasted pecans and fold them through.

Pour the mixture into your prepared pastry case, then top with the remaining whole pecans. Place in the oven for 30 to 35 minutes, or until set through. Keep a close eye on the tart. If it begins to brown too quickly, just cover it with aluminum foil.

For the custard, whisk together the egg yolks, cornstarch, milk, sugar and bourbon in a small saucepan. Add the reserved vanilla pod and continue whisking whilst slowly bringing the mixture to a simmer over a low heat. Once thickened, remove the custard from the heat, discard the vanilla pod and pour it into a jug to stop the cooking process.

Pour the warm custard over your perfectly sliced tart.

5. Sensational Scones, Biscuits and Slices

If you're new to baking, these delicious and simple recipes are a great place to start. Whether you plan to bake cookies, scones or slices, this chapter has plenty of recipes to help.

Scones and cookies (or biscuits) are small baked goods, simple mixtures of fat, flour, liquid and a leavener such as baking powder or baking soda (called bicarb soda in Australia). In most English-speaking countries except for the United States, crunchy cookies are called biscuits. However, chewier biscuits are sometimes called cookies in Australia and the United Kingdom. A "slice" is not, as many Americans think, a wedge of pizza, but rather a usually layered confection served in a rectangular portion, which in the United States is often called a bar. Whatever they are called, they will reliably please.

There's no more joyful way to spend an afternoon than baking. From Fluffy Lemonade Scones (page 107) to Extra Chewy ANZAC Biscuits (page 111) to the Caramel, Peanut and Chocolate Slice (page 122), there is something in this chapter for you! These simple but brilliant baking recipes are no frills, no fuss—just downright delicious.

Fluffy Lemonade Scones

Makes 10 to 12 scones

3 cups (375 g) self-rising flour

1 cup (240 ml) fresh good-quality cream or heavy cream

1 cup (240 ml) lemonade soda, sweet

1 tsp vanilla extract

Optional Flavor Variants

1 cup (175 g) chopped dates

½ cup (74 g) fresh blueberries and ½ cup (90 g) white chocolate chips

½ cup (80 g) golden raisins

½ cup (15 g) chopped fresh spinach and ¼ cup (38 g) crumbled feta

Toppings

Whipping or thickened cream

Basic Berry Jam (page 30)

Unsalted butter

I've come to appreciate scones for their simplicity, texture and purpose. To me, a scone is a baked pillow, the perfect vessel to hold jam and cream. Although in the recipe below I use standard measurements, know that Nan would only use a mug from her cupboard that she called her scone mug.

Nan's scones are now a staple at Cakeboi. Through trial and error, a staff member, Wyatt, has perfected these scones, replicating them as if Nan baked them herself. At Cakeboi, we bake them fresh and serve them hot from the oven. They are lucky to last an hour because everyone loves scones.

Preheat the oven to 390°F (200°C) and line a baking tray with baking paper.

To start the scones, sift self-rising flour into a large mixing bowl. In a separate bowl, mix together the cream, lemonade soda and vanilla, then pour the sifted flour over it. This is where you can add some optional flavors. Now, using a butter knife, mix the ingredients together until the scone dough forms, and then turn it out onto a lightly floured work surface. Lightly knead the dough for about two or three turns, or until it just comes together.

Roll the dough into a large round disk about 2 inches (5 cm) thick. Now, using a 2-inch (5-cm) ring cutter, cut out scones. Ensure you dip the cutter into flour each time you shape a scone to keep the dough from sticking.

Place the scones on the baking tray, just touching each other. Then put them into the oven for 15 minutes, or until golden.

Top with the best quality semi-whipped cream and some of your favorite jam, or with some butter for a more savory treat.

Tips and Tricks: For the perfect dairy-free scone, just replace the cream with coconut cream. The fattiness of the coconut cream creates such a beautiful scone, the texture is to die for.

Nan's Pumpkin Scones with Whipped Maple Butter

Makes 8 scones

½ cup (120 g) butter, at room temperature

½ cup (110 g) caster sugar

2 eggs, at room temperature

½ cup (120 g) pureed cooked pumpkin

3 cups (375 g) self-rising flour

Whipped Maple Butter

⅔ cup (150 g) butter

⅓ cup (80 ml) maple syrup

Pinch of salt

Tip: When making scones it is best to work the dough with a butter knife rather than a spoon. This will prevent the dough from being overworked as the knife cuts through the flour whilst combining the ingredients.

How do you make scones even better? Easy, add pumpkin. Pumpkin is something I use a lot in baking. It has a beautiful sweet savory flavor. In this recipe, it enhances the simplicity of traditional scones by taking you to another delicious dimension of delight. Dab whipped maple butter on this delectable dish to add extra elegance. Go from a drab brunch to a fab long lunch, as these treats are key to perfecting morning tea!

For the scones, use a large mixing bowl and beat the butter and sugar with an electric mixer until light and pale. Add the eggs one at a time and beat until each egg is fully incorporated. Now stir in the pumpkin, then sift in the self-rising flour. Switch to a butter knife and mix the ingredients with it until the scone dough comes together (see Tip). Turn out the dough onto a lightly floured work surface, then very lightly knead the dough for about two or three turns, or until it just comes together.

Roll the dough into an even thickness of about 2 inches (5 cm). To shape the scones, use a 2-inch (5-cm) ring cutter. Ensure you dip the cutter into flour each time you shape a scone to keep the dough from sticking.

Position the scones on a baking tray so that they are just touching each other. Now put them into the oven for 15 minutes, or until they are golden.

Whilst the scones are baking, make the whipped maple butter. In a large mixing bowl, beat the butter with an electric mixer on a medium-high speed until it is light and fluffy. Add the maple syrup and salt, and beat again on a medium-high speed until well combined.

Serve the whipped maple butter with the warm scones fresh out of the oven.

Extra Chewy ANZAC Biscuits (Bikkies)

Makes 8 to 10 biscuits

½ cup (125 g) butter

2½ oz (75 ml) golden syrup

¾ cup (150 g) brown sugar

1 cup (125 g) self-rising flour

2 cups (200 g) rolled oats

1¼ cups (115 g) shredded coconut

2 tbsp (30 ml) boiling water

1 tsp baking soda

½ tsp salt

Tips and Tricks: Hannah, a staff member and best friend of ten years, takes these cookies home and heats them up in the microwave before eating them. Even though they are delicious fresh, she believes heating turns them gooey, which makes them become a delicious after-dinner dessert.

The crunchiness of ANZAC biscuits dates back to the early 1900s when they were invented. It was said that soldiers' wives needed a recipe that would stay fresh for months, so they could send them overseas. Apparently some of these biscuits were so hard that soldiers ground them up into porridge just to eat them. Nan would bake ANZAC biscuits for the markets; however, hers were always really flat and crisp. I have adjusted this recipe to allow for a more chewy and pleasurable experience—don't worry, you won't need to grind mine into porridge.

At Cakeboi we have ANZAC Bikkies in our display cabinet every day. The aroma of a tray full of freshly baked goodies sends our customers into a purchasing frenzy. Our ANZAC Bikkies are our most common accompaniment to a takeaway coffee.

To start the ANZAC biscuits, preheat a fan forced oven to 355°F (180°C) or a non-convection oven to 385°F (195°C). Heat the butter, golden syrup and brown sugar in a small saucepan over a medium heat until the butter is melted. Remove the pan from the heat and leave until it is needed.

Mix together the self-rising flour, rolled oats and coconut in a large mixing bowl. In a separate small bowl, stir together the boiling water, baking soda and salt. Pour the baking soda paste into the melted butter and then whisk it as it foams up. Now add the butter mixture to the dry ingredients and mix everything together.

To make small cookies, use a levelled scoop from a tablespoon (15 g). To make larger cookies, use ¼ cup (60 g) of the dough and roll into a ball. Press the dough balls out into disks about ¾ inch (2 cm) thick, then place them on baking trays lined with baking paper, at least 2 inches (5 cm) apart.

Bake the smaller bikkies for 12 to 14 minutes and the larger ones for 18 to 20 minutes, or until the bikkies are evenly golden. Cool them completely before eating them.

Passionfruit Custard Slice

Makes 12 slices

1 serving Rough Puff Pastry (page 26)

Custard Filling

1 cup (220 g) caster sugar

1 cup (150 g) custard powder

10 tbsp (75 g) cornstarch

6 cups (1440 ml) milk

2 cups (480 ml) thickened cream or heavy cream

¼ cup (60 g) butter

2 egg yolks

2 tsp (10 ml) vanilla extract

What could be better than a creamy vanilla custard slice?

The vanilla slice is a staple of bakeries in Australia, and everyone claims to have the best recipe, but Cakeboi's might just take the cake (or slice). This irresistible dessert has vanilla custard sandwiched between layers of flaky, buttery puff pastry, and its tangy passionfruit icing has a sharpness that balances the richness of the pastry and custard.

This old-fashioned passionfruit custard slice is bound to be a hit with the whole family.

Prepare your Rough Puff Pastry dough as per page 26.

Preheat the oven to 425°F (220°C), then line two large trays with baking paper. Divide your pastry in two, then roll each out into a square about ⅛ inch (4 mm) thick. Place the pastry on the large baking trays and bake them for 20 minutes, or until they are evenly golden. Allow them to cool to room temperature.

Line a 12 x 12–inch (30 x 30–cm) square tin with baking paper, make sure there is enough paper to go up the sides and over the lip of the tin. Trim the pastry so it will neatly fit into the tin.

To cook the custard, mix together the sugar, custard powder and cornstarch in a bowl. Add one-third of the milk, then whisk to create a paste with no lumps. Add the remaining milk and the cream to the mixture, whisk it until it is smooth, then place it in a large saucepan.

Bring the mixture to a boil, then cook it for 3 minutes, or until it is super thick and no longer has a floury taste. Remove it from the heat, then add the butter, egg yolks and vanilla. Now whisk to combine all the ingredients.

To assemble the slice, place one trimmed sheet of pastry in the prepared baking tin, followed by the custard. Place the other layer of pastry on top of the custard, then lightly press it down so that there is no air between the layers. Place the tin in the refrigerator for at least 4 hours or overnight until the custard is firmly set.

Passionfruit Icing

1⅔ cups (240 g) icing sugar mixture (page 14)

2 tsp (10 g) butter, melted

2 tsp (8 g) passionfruit pulp

2 tsp (10 ml) water

To make the passionfruit icing, mix together the icing sugar mixture, butter and passionfruit pulp in a small heatproof bowl. Add the water, then stir it to form a paste-like icing. Place the bowl over a saucepan of simmering water, stirring for 2 to 3 minutes until the mixture slowly runs down the back of a spoon. Now ice the top layer of the slice. Chill it for 20 minutes, or until the icing sets.

Remove the slice from the tin and cut it, as we do at Cakeboi, into a dozen 3 x 4-inch (8 x 10-cm) portions, or, depending on your mood and the crowd, into sixteen 3-inch (8-cm) squares or even nine 4-inch (10-cm) squares.

Lemon Zest and Passionfruit Melting Moments

**Makes 8 biscuits
(16 halves)**

½ cup (125 g) unsalted butter, at room temperature

1 tsp vanilla extract

1 tsp lemon zest

2 tbsp (20 g) icing sugar

1 scant cup (115 g) all-purpose flour

5 tbsp (40 g) cornstarch

Passionfruit Vienna Cream

¼ cup (60 g) unsalted butter, at room temperature

1 cup (140 g) icing sugar

2 tsp (8 g) passionfruit pulp

Icing sugar, for decorating

This recipe came to me through a good friend of mine, Teresa. She is the most hilarious woman you will ever meet. During lockdown Teresa became quite the amateur baker and acquired this recipe from her partner Peter (I call him Poita). This is Peter's mother's old recipe. I have the original still in her handwriting. I've just added my own touches here and there.

Melting Moments are soft and sweet and can be made with many different flavors. Traditionally, the most common and classic flavored center is a tangy lemon buttercream. It is definitely the flavor combo that I enjoy the most. However, my mother was obsessed with passionfruit filling. So, are you Team Lemon or Team Passionfruit? Why pick sides? At my bakery, Cakeboi, I decided to combine these two iconic flavors. So I created a lemon zest shortbread with a passionfruit Vienna cream icing—you're welcome! Just try and stop at one. Sorry, not sorry.

To start, preheat the oven to 320°F (160°C), then grease two oven trays and line them with baking paper. Place the butter, vanilla, lemon zest and icing sugar in a bowl and beat them with an electric mixer until the butter lightens in color. Sift in the flour and the cornstarch, then fold them through the butter mixture.

Roll two levelled teaspoons into one ball of dough for each biscuit, then arrange the balls on the baking tray 2 inches (5 cm) apart. Lightly press them with a floured fork, then place in the oven for 12 minutes, or until lightly golden. Remove the biscuits from the oven and place them on a cooling rack.

For the passionfruit Vienna cream, place the butter, icing sugar and passionfruit pulp in a small bowl, then beat with an electric mixer until light and fluffy.

To assemble, dollop a tablespoon of the icing between two rolled biscuits, then repeat until all the biscuits are filled. Lightly dust the Melting Moments with icing sugar before serving.

The Classic Monte Carlo Biscuit

Makes 10 biscuits (20 halves)

Monte Carlos are two delicious, chewy coconut biscuit shells that are sandwiched together, filled with cream and a dollop of sticky raspberry jam. They're my absolute all-time childhood favorite biscuits. In fact, my dogs are named Monty (exciting, playful and welcoming) and Carlo (sweet, simple and flaky) because they reflect these biscuits perfectly.

¾ cup + 1 tbsp (185 g) unsalted butter, softened

½ cup (110 g) caster sugar

1 tsp vanilla extract

2 tbsp (30 ml) honey

1 egg, at room temperature

1½ cups (185 g) self-rising flour, sifted

1 scant cup (115 g) all-purpose flour, sifted

½ cup (40 g) desiccated coconut

Preheat the oven to 340°F (170°C) and line two baking trays with baking paper. In a large mixing bowl, place the butter, sugar, vanilla and honey. Beat it all with an electric mixer on high for approximately 1 minute to cream the ingredients. Add the room-temperature egg, then mix on a medium speed for 1 minute more. Add both flours and coconut to the wet ingredients and fold through until well combined. Divide the dough into two, then roll it out into logs about 2 inches (5 cm) thick and wrap them in cling wrap. Place the dough logs in the refrigerator for 15 to 20 minutes to firm up.

Remove the cling wrap, then cut ½-inch (1.3-cm) disks out of the dough. Place the dough disks on the baking paper, then place in the hot oven for 15 minutes, or until golden. Allow the biscuits to cool on the tray before moving.

Vanilla Buttercream

1 cup + 1 tbsp (240 g) butter, softened

4 cups (560 g) icing sugar

4 tsp (20 ml) milk

1 tsp vanilla extract

For the vanilla buttercream, place the softened butter, icing sugar, milk and vanilla in a medium-sized mixing bowl, then beat with an electric mixer on high until light and fluffy.

To assemble the Monte Carlo, sandwich two biscuits with a tablespoon of buttercream and a teaspoon of jam. Dust with icing sugar.

½ cup (160 g) raspberry Basic Berry Jam (page 30)

2 tbsp (20 g) icing sugar

Jam Drops

Makes 16 biscuits

¾ cup (180 g) butter, at room
temperature

1 cup + 1 tbsp (240 g) caster
sugar

1 tsp vanilla extract

Zest of ½ orange

1 egg

2⅓ cups (300 g) self-rising flour

3 tbsp (50 g) Basic Berry Jam
(page 30)

Jam drops are a classic family favorite. These old-fashioned sweets are the most delicious melt-in-your-mouth thumbprint cookies ever. They are soft and buttery vanilla biscuits topped with a sweet berry jam filling. You can fill these delicious biscuits with a dollop of your favorite type of jam.

They also make a great activity for kids, because it's so simple! Get them to help measure the ingredients, roll the cookie dough and press the centers.

Whip up these simple jam drops in minutes. I doubt they'll remain in the cookie jar for long, though.

Preheat the oven to 340°F (170°C) fan forced, or, for a non-convection oven, 365°F (185°C). Prepare a baking tray lined with baking paper.

Place the butter, sugar, vanilla and orange zest in a small mixing bowl. With a mixer fitted with a paddle attachment, cream the butter and sugar until light and fluffy. Add the egg, then continue to beat until the mixture is well incorporated and has smoothed out.

Sift the self-rising flour, then fold it through the mixture with a wooden spoon until no flour lumps remain.

Use a dessert spoon (about 2 tsp [10 ml]) to shape the dough into rounds. Space them out over the baking tray, allowing enough room for the cookies to spread. Indent a fingerprint into the top of the balls, about half the depth of the dough. Dollop ½ teaspoon of jam in the middle.

Place the tray in the oven, then bake for 10 to 12 minutes, or until the sides start to golden.

Cherry Ripe Slice

**Makes 1 tray or
12 small slices**

*Cherry Ripes are truly iconic chocolate bars in Australia, and
fans of traditional Cherry Ripe will love this classic "homemade"
combination. It has cherry and coconut on top of a crisp chocolate
base and is topped with a thick layer of melted chocolate.*

*This was another recipe that Nan would make for her weekly
markets. It was a big favorite of mine as a child. I would always
try and save a tray for myself.*

*The Cherry Ripe Slice is the perfect way to satisfy your sweet
cravings, and it makes the perfect afternoon treat. It is Cherr-ific!*

Base

1 scant cup (200 g) butter,
melted

1½ cups (190 g) self-rising flour

1 cup (90 g) desiccated coconut

¼ cup (50 g) brown sugar

¼ cup (55 g) raw sugar

Filling

1 (14-oz [395-g]) tin condensed
milk

⅔ cup (150 g) finely chopped
glacéed cherries , see Tips and
Tricks

3 cups (280 g) desiccated
coconut

½ cup (100 g) Copha or
vegetable shortening, melted

2 drops pink food dye (optional)

Topping

7 oz (200 g) milk chocolate,
chopped

2 tbsp (30 ml) vegetable oil

Preheat the oven to 355°F (180°C) and lightly grease an 8 x 10–inch
(20 x 30–cm) slice tin or baking pan, then line it with baking paper.
Ensure that the baking paper runs up the sides of the tin. This
allows for the extra paper to be used as handles when removing
the set slice.

For the base of this slice, simply mix together the melted butter
with the self-rising flour, coconut, brown sugar and raw sugar. Now
press the mixture into the base of your prepared slice tin. Place it
in the oven to bake for 20 to 25 minutes, or until evenly golden.

For the filling, in a large bowl mix together the condensed milk,
cherries, coconut, melted Copha and pink food dye until all the
ingredients are evenly coated. Pour the filling onto the cooked base
in the tin and lightly spread it with a spoon. Now place it in the
refrigerator for 1 hour to set.

For the topping, melt the chocolate in a heatproof bowl over a
small saucepan of boiling water. Add the vegetable oil and mix
it through. Pour the chocolate evenly over the filling and spread it
to all the corners. Place the tin back in the refrigerator for another
1 hour to set the contents before slicing.

Tips and Tricks: In this recipe we use glacéed cherries,
which are a "candied cherry." These are similar to a maraschino
cherry; however, they are processed a little bit longer to create
a more confectionery-style cherry. They are often found in the
supermarket with the dried fruit.

Caramel, Peanut and Chocolate Slice

Makes 1 tray or 12 small slices

Caramel, peanut butter and chocolate—is there a more enticing combination? It's a classic, and this is another treat that brings back the wonder of childhood. The salted peanuts help to cut through its intense sweetness and add a lovely crunch.

The best way to get through the week is to have something truly delicious in the middle of it. This slice is it!

Base

¼ cup (50 g) crushed peanuts

¼ cup (60 g) butter, melted

1 cup (125 g) all-purpose flour

1 cup (90 g) desiccated coconut

½ cup (110 g) raw sugar

Preheat the oven to 355°F (180°C) and lightly grease an 8 x 10–inch (20 x 30–cm) slice tin or baking pan, then line it with baking paper. Ensure that the baking paper runs up the sides of the tin. This allows for the extra paper to be used as handles when removing the set slice.

For the base of this slice, firstly I like to break the peanuts down even more. Place them on a clean tea towel, then fold the towel to cover the nuts. Roll a rolling pin over the towel to crush the nuts. Now mix together the melted butter with the flour, coconut, sugar and nuts. Press the mixture into the base of your prepared slice tin, then place in the oven to bake for 15 to 20 minutes, or until evenly golden.

Filling

1 (14-oz [395-g]) tin condensed milk

¼ cup (60 ml) golden syrup

7 tbsp (100 g) butter, melted

Pinch of salt

To make the filling, place the condensed milk, golden syrup, melted butter and salt in a small saucepan, then heat the mixture, stirring it to loosen. Pour it over the cooked tart base, then place the tin back in the oven for 15 minutes. Remove the slice from the oven, then place it on a rack to cool to room temperature.

Topping

7 oz (200 g) dark chocolate

2 tbsp (30 ml) vegetable oil

For the topping, melt the chocolate in a heatproof bowl over a small saucepan of boiling water. Add the oil and mix it through. Pour the chocolate evenly over the filling and spread it to all the corners. Place the tin in the refrigerator for 1 hour to set the contents before slicing.

Nan's Cornflake Biscuits

Makes 12 biscuits

½ cup (110 g) caster sugar (raw caster sugar if you can find it)

½ cup (110 g) unsalted butter, at room temperature

3 tbsp (45 ml) honey

1 egg, at room temperature

½ cup (80 g) golden raisins

1 cup (125 g) self-rising flour

¼ cup (50 g) crushed peanuts

3 cups (85 g) cornflakes, divided

This was my number-one favorite biscuit that my nan would make me as a child. Super delicious, soft and crunchy.

I attempted Nan's old recipe and adapted it with a crushed nut flavor, opting to keep the raisins, which give the needed burst of sweetness. This delicious, nutty, crunchy and soft biscuit will have you coming back for more.

Preheat the oven to 320°F (160°C) fan forced, or, for a non-convection oven, 345°F (175°C). Prepare two large baking trays lined with baking paper.

To start the biscuit, cream together the sugar, butter and honey with an electric mixer fitted with a paddle attachment. Once light and fluffy, add the egg, then beat until fully incorporated. Using a wooden spoon, gently mix through the golden raisins, self-rising flour, crushed peanuts and 2 cups (57 g) of the cornflakes.

Place the remaining 1 cup (28 g) of cornflakes in a shallow bowl. Scoop a dessert spoonful (about 2 tsp [10 ml]) of dough and roll it into a ball. Roll the ball in the additional cornflakes to coat the dough. Repeat until all the dough is used.

Space the dough balls out over the baking trays, allowing enough room for the biscuits to spread. Lightly press the dough with the back of a fork, then place the trays in the oven for 20 minutes.

Transfer to a cooling rack and allow the biscuits to come to room temperature to set.

Milo and Caramel Brownie

Makes 1 brownie tray or 8 slices

1 (14-oz [395-g]) tin Caramelized Condensed Milk (page 14)

1 scant cup (200 g) butter

7 oz (200 g) bittersweet (around 50%) chocolate

¼ cup (60 g) Milo (chocolate-flavored malted beverage powder)

3 eggs

⅔ cup (150 g) brown sugar

2 tsp (10 ml) vanilla extract

½ cup (60 g) self-rising flour

⅓ cup (30 g) cocoa powder

Pinch of salt

Do you remember enjoying a glass of Milo as a kid? This delicious dessert will walk you back down memory lane!

I can honestly say that I've never tried a brownie combination that I didn't like. If you love regular chocolate brownies like me, then you are going to absolutely love these Milo brownies. They are soft and fudgy, with a delicious taste, and adding Milo gives them the most amazing texture.

This simple Milo and Caramel Brownie recipe contains a few pantry staples, so they are easy and convenient to make. They are so good, it will be hard to stop at just one.

Prepare the caramelized condensed milk as per page 14, and allow it to cool.

Preheat the oven to 340°F (170°C). Prepare an 8-inch (20-cm) square brownie tin with grease and baking paper.

Place the butter, chocolate and Milo in a heatproof bowl. Heat over a pot of simmering water, continually stirring until the butter and chocolate are both completely melted. Remove the bowl from the heat and allow it to slightly cool. Add the eggs one at a time to the warm chocolate, vigorously whisking, not moving on to the next until the previous one is fully incorporated. Add the sugar and vanilla, then whisk until well combined.

Sift the self-rising flour, cocoa powder and salt into the wet mixture. Gently mix through until there are no lumps remaining.

Dollop spoons of the caramelized condensed milk around the bottom of the tray, then pour your brownie batter into the tray, or dollop the caramelized condensed milk on top after you have poured the batter. Place the brownies in the oven to cook for 15 to 20 minutes, then cool them in the fridge for at least 3 hours or until set.

Classic Pumpkin Loaf

Makes 1 loaf

1 (1.1-lb [500-g]) pumpkin quarter

½ cup (120 ml) olive oil, divided

2 eggs

¾ cup + 1 tbsp (165 g) sugar

⅓ cup (80 g) brown sugar

1 tsp salt

1 tsp vanilla extract

2⅓ cups (300 g) self-rising flour

1 tbsp (8 g) cinnamon

1 tbsp (8 g) cardamom

¼ cup (25 g) pumpkin seeds or crushed walnuts, to sprinkle on the top

I love pumpkin season; pumpkin is my favorite vegetable to bake with. During this season I make pumpkin flavored EVERYTHING!

Pumpkin bread brings a real sense of home; the fragrance floods my mind with warm memories. This classic treat is a dream worth waking up to. There is nothing cozier than cupping your hands around a coffee whilst enjoying this breakfast bread.

This recipe secured my first immunity win on MasterChef. I believe the odds were in my favor because this recipe is irresistible. It is a delicious balance of amazing texture and flavor that isn't too sweet.

To make this loaf, preheat the oven to 340°F (170°C) and line a 4 x 8–inch (10 x 20–cm) loaf tin with baking paper.

Cut the pumpkin into ¼-inch (6-mm) cubes then place on a roasting tray lined with baking paper. Give the pumpkin cubes a light oiling with 1 tablespoon (15 ml) of the olive oil, then place them in the oven for 20 minutes, or until they are soft. Try not to brown the pumpkin. Remove it from the oven, discarding the pumpkin skin, then puree it using a masher and set it aside for later.

Place the eggs, both sugars, salt and vanilla in a bowl then mix it to combine it all. Add the remaining olive oil and the pumpkin, then mix it well. Finally, add the flour, cinnamon and cardamom, and mix until no lumps remain.

Pour the mixture into the lined tin, sprinkle with either pumpkin seeds or crushed walnuts, then place into the oven. Bake for 50 to 60 minutes, or until a skewer inserted in the center comes out clean.

Let the bread cool for a few hours before slicing it; otherwise it will crumble and not be as moist.

Tips and Tricks: You can add a mix of different spices, such as nutmeg and clove, if you prefer.

6. Yeast Bakes

Regardless of whether you're new to baking or a pro at it, it's important to understand how yeast works. Yeast is a living organism; therefore, it needs food and moisture to thrive. Baker's yeast feeds on sugar and converts it to carbon dioxide through fermentation. When water and sugar are added to yeast, the carbon dioxide created is responsible for stretching and expanding the dough. This is why dough rises. During this process of yeast fermentation, the flavor and texture you expect is created.

It is important to let the dough rest after working or shaping it. Cover the dough with a clean towel or plastic wrap and set it aside for 10 to 15 minutes. Allowing the dough to relax and settle results in voluminous dough that becomes easier to shape.

Don't be intimidated by baking with yeast. Some people find it scary and yeast recipes arduous and complicated. But yeast is just another ingredient in the bowl. Let your confidence build with these delicious yeast recipes. I suggest starting with the Spiced Rum Baba (page 133). It will get you addicted to yeast bakes.

Some handy tips:

- I keep my yeast in the freezer. A chef once told me this keeps it in its prime for longer. Seems to work for me. At the shop we go through a lot of yeast, but whilst writing this book I found an old container of yeast in my freezer that is at least two years old. I used it, and it worked perfectly.

- Proof dough in a warm, moist environment. Do not let your dough dry out, or it will form cracks when it's baking. I have a spray bottle filled with water that I use to mist the dough if I feel it is drying out.

- Get comfortable feeling the textures of the process. Appreciate the smooth well-kneaded dough, start to understand the feel of a proofed dough and one that is underproofed. A proofed dough is light and airy (if you poke it, it will jiggle) whereas an underproofed dough is dense.

Spiced Rum Baba

Makes 6 individual
cakes

This recipe is pure joy. It represents one of my favorite memories on MasterChef. This is the dessert I cooked for Katy Perry. One bite sent her into a rhythmic motion followed by those famous words, "You're the tits, Reece." Rum baba is a rum-soaked yeast cake that is part of a larger family of alcohol-soaked cakes known as babas or babkas. The story goes, Stanislaus I, after a long journey, thought the babka cake was too dry, so he decided to sweeten and moisten it with some alcohol and, well, that's how this party started!

3 eggs

2 tsp (7 g) yeast

2 tsp (8 g) sugar

1 cup (125 g) all-purpose flour

4½ tbsp (65 g) butter, melted

Preheat the oven to 355°F (180°C), and grease the baba molds with spray oil. (Rum baba is usually baked in a mini Bundt pan tray. If you're unable to find one of these, just use a small cupcake tray.)

Rum Syrup

1⅔ cups (375 g) caster sugar

½ cup (120 ml) spiced rum

2 cups (480 ml) water

3 black peppercorns

½ vanilla bean

To prepare the baba batter, whisk together the eggs, yeast and sugar in a bowl. Add the flour and knead it in with an electric mixer fitted with a dough hook attachment for approximately 5 minutes, or until the mixture is soft and elastic. Remember to scrape the bowl down as you go. Add the melted butter, then knead again for an additional 5 minutes so it incorporates.

Divide the dough between the greased molds using dessert spoons (2 teaspoons [10 ml]) or a piping bag.. Cover the tray in a tea towel and place it in a warm place to proof for 30 minutes, or until it doubles in size. Then place in the oven and bake for 15 to 20 minutes, or until the cakes are golden.

*Orange and Vanilla
Chantilly Cream*

1 cup (240 ml) thickened or whipping cream

4 tbsp (30 g) icing sugar, sifted

Zest of 1 orange

½ vanilla bean

Once baked, allow the cakes to cool completely before soaking them in the syrup.

To make the rum syrup, place the caster sugar, rum, water, peppercorns and half vanilla pod with the seeds in a saucepan and whisk them together, then bring the mixture to a boil. Boil the syrup for 5 minutes to infuse the flavors. Remove it from the heat and cool it completely before dropping the babas into the syrup and allowing them to soak for 10 minutes. Once the babas are soaked, remove them from the syrup and set them on a tray, ready to decorate.

Tips and Tricks: This recipe is written for six because, like most baked goods, babas are best when freshly made. But if you have more than six dinner guests, by all means double the quantities.

For the Chantilly cream, place the cream, icing sugar and orange zest in a bowl, scrape the seeds out of the half vanilla pod and add them to the cream, then whisk it all together until soft peaks are formed. Dollop the orange cream on top of each soaked rum baba.

1 serving Pastry Cream (page 37)

¾ cup (180 ml) milk

1 tsp vanilla extract

½ cup (110 g) caster sugar

2 tsp (7 g) dried yeast

2½ cups (315 g) all-purpose flour

2 eggs, at room temperature

7 tbsp (100 g) butter, softened

Vegetable oil spray

Topping

⅓ cup (70 g) butter

¼ cup (60 g) caster sugar

⅓ cup (80 ml) honey

1 cup (120 g) flaked almonds

Pinch of salt

Icing sugar, for decorating

This traditional German treat is a double-layered brioche cake that is oozing with a thick, rich vanilla cream and crowned by a crunchy, gooey honey-almond topping. Its proper name is Bienenstich, which translates to Bee Sting. The dessert originated in Germany, but it has become a popular staple in Australian bakeries. If you love honey and almonds, this classic treat will have you buzzing with joy! I guarantee this is one bee sting you'll be glad to receive.

Prepare the pastry cream as per page 37.

Start the brioche at least 3 hours before you want to bake it. Place your milk and vanilla in a small saucepan, then on a low heat bring it to a simmer. Remove the pan from the heat and set it aside for 5 minutes.

In the bowl of a stand mixer, place your caster sugar, dried yeast and flour. Add the warm milk and, with an electric mixer fitted with a dough hook attachment, knead on a low speed. Add the eggs one at a time, then turn the mixer up to a medium-high speed to ensure everything is well incorporated. Add the butter, then knead until there are no lumps remaining.

Reduce the speed back to low and continue to knead the dough for 5 to 6 minutes. Once it is smooth and elastic, grease the top with spray vegetable oil, then cover it with a damp cloth. Leave the dough to double in size for about 1 hour.

Whilst the dough is rising, prepare your topping. In a small saucepan heat together your butter, sugar and honey until the sugar is dissolved. Remove from the heat, then add your flaked almonds and salt, stir to combine, then set aside.

Preheat the oven to 355°F (180°C). Grease and line an 8-inch (20-cm) springform baking tin with baking paper. Knock the air out of the dough by rolling it on a lightly floured surface into a ball, then place it in the center of the tin. Cover it with a damp cloth and leave until doubled in size. Pour the almond mixture over the top of the dough.

Bake the dough for 30 minutes, or until golden all over and firm in the middle. Run a knife around the inside of the tin, then gently pop the spring of the tin. Leave the brioche on a wire rack until completely cooled.

Carefully cut horizontally through the middle of the brioche, then dollop the pastry cream on the bottom half. Spread the pastry cream to the edges, then place the other layer on top, and finish by dusting it with icing sugar.

Bee Sting with Vanilla Pastry Cream

Baked Rhubarb, Tonka Bean and Brioche Tartlets

Makes 12 tartlets

Rhubarb and tonka bean custard is a classic pairing. The custard calms and balances the bold sharpness of the rhubarb. They are a delicious match made in heaven.

3½ cups (445 g) bread flour (all-purpose flour is also okay)

2 tsp (7 g) yeast

½ cup (120 g) caster sugar, divided

Pinch of salt

½ cup (120 ml) milk

3 whole eggs

1 scant cup (200 g) butter, cubed, not cold but firm enough to hold its shape

1 whole tonka bean

Vegetable oil spray

1 serving Pastry Cream (page 37)

1 bunch rhubarb

1 cup (200 g) Demerara sugar

Start this recipe the day before you want to bake the tartlets. In the bowl of a stand mixer, sift together your flour, yeast, ¼ cup (60 g) of caster sugar and salt, then add your milk and eggs. With a dough hook attachment, knead the dough for 8 minutes. Remember to scrape down the sides if needed. When the dough looks elastic and smooth, start to feed in the butter, one cube at a time. Knead it for an additional 10 minutes, then place the dough in a greased bowl, cover it with plastic wrap, and rest it in the refrigerator overnight.

Whilst the dough is resting, prepare the pastry cream as per page 37, replacing the vanilla with finely grated tonka bean.

On the second day, remove the brioche dough from the fridge and, using a bench knife, divide it into twelve equal portions. Shape each portion into a ball, then roll it into a disk ½ inch (1.3 cm) thick. Lightly grease your tartlet tins or large muffin tins. Now place the dough disks in the tins. Ensure that the cups of the tins are lined with the dough coming up the sides. Spray the dough with oil, cover with a damp cloth, then leave to rise until they begin to puff. This should take about 30 minutes.

In the meantime, prepare your rhubarb by slicing it into batons that are nearly 1 inch (2.5 cm) shorter than the diameter of your tartlet tins. Line them up on a baking tray, sprinkle with the remaining ¼ cup (60 g) of caster sugar, and then bake for 8 minutes. Once they are cooked, place them on a wire rack to cool, and reserve the excess juices.

To assemble your tartlets, dollop 1 tablespoon (15 ml) of pastry cream in the middle of each brioche, then place three rhubarb batons on the pastry cream, and sprinkle the edges of the brioche with the Demerara sugar.

Bake the tartlets for 20 minutes, or until they are evenly golden. Brush the excess juices onto the rhubarb as the tartlets cool.

Simple Donuts

Makes 12 donuts

Who can resist soft and fluffy donuts? These perfect yeast donuts are easy to make, and they'll have you jumping for joy.

These homemade donuts are enticing. This recipe is best for sugared, cream- or jam-filled donuts. It will result in a truly great, hot, crisp donut. Once you've mastered this basic recipe for a fluffy, yeasted donut, you won't need to visit a donut shop ever again.

⅔ cup (160 ml) water

4 tsp (14 g) yeast

½ cup (100 g) sugar

7 oz (200 ml) milk, at room temperature

Pinch of salt

1 cup (220 g) butter, at room temperature

2 eggs, at room temperature

5¾ cups (720 g) all-purpose flour, sifted

4 cups (960 ml) vegetable oil, for frying, plus more for brushing on the donuts

2 cups (440 g) caster sugar

1 cup (280 g) Basic Berry Jam (page 30) or Pastry Cream (page 37)

To start the dough, mix the water, yeast and a pinch of your weighed-out sugar in a bowl, then leave the mixture for 5 minutes for the yeast to activate. The yeast will become light and foamy.

Place the remaining sugar, milk, salt and butter in a small saucepan, and heat it over a low heat until the butter is melted. Remove it from the heat, then pour the mixture into a large mixing bowl. Allow it to cool to room temperature before adding the eggs, the activated yeast and the sifted flour. Using a wooden spoon, bring all the ingredients together to form a dough.

Turn the dough out onto a lightly floured work surface. Knead the dough for 10 minutes, or until it has a smooth surface and springs back when lightly poked. Place the dough in a lightly greased mixing bowl, then cover it with a damp tea towel. Leave the dough to double in size, which will take about 1 hour.

Turn the dough out again onto a lightly floured work surface, then roll it until it is a scant 1 inch (2.5 cm) thick. Using a ring cutter with a diameter of about 2½ inches (6 cm), cut your donuts out of the dough and place them on a lined baking tray. Brush the donuts with vegetable oil, then cover them with a damp tea towel and leave them until they become plump and fluffy. This should take about 40 minutes.

Place the caster sugar in a bowl. Heat the vegetable oil to 355°F (180°C), then carefully cook the donuts in the oil for 1 minute on each side. As they come out of the oil, toss the hot donuts in the sugar.

Once they are cooled and easier to handle, fill a piping bag with jam or pastry cream. Insert the tip of the bag into each donut and pipe in your chosen filling.

Nostalgic Finger Buns

Makes 12 buns

4 cups (550 g) bread flour

⅓ cup (75 g) caster sugar

¼ cup (60 g) butter, softened

2 eggs, at room temperature

4 tsp (14 g) yeast

Pinch of salt

5 oz (150 ml) milk, at room temperature

5 oz (150 ml) water

Vegetable oil spray

Egg Wash

1 egg

1 tsp milk

Filling

1 serving Basic Berry Jam (page 30)

1 serving Pastry Cream (page 37) or whipped cream

½ cup (70 g) icing sugar

Growing up, I remember staring into the glass display cabinet at a bakery, yearning for a delicious finger bun. Sometimes we would take these to school as a treat. If you've ever wanted to relive your childhood, then this recipe is for you, for you shall make your own and eat as many as you like!

You can pick and choose your toppings or add raisins for a more traditional finger bun. Regardless of what you choose, these finger buns are a real winner.

To start the dough, sift the flour into a large mixing bowl, then add the sugar, butter, eggs, yeast, salt, milk and water. Stir with a wooden spoon until a dough ball begins to form.

Turn the dough out onto a lightly floured work surface. Knead for 10 minutes, or until the dough has a smooth surface and springs back when it is poked. Place the dough in a lightly greased mixing bowl, then cover it with a damp tea towel. Leave the dough to double in size, which will take about 1 hour.

Roll the dough into a log about 12 inches (30 cm) long, then cut it into twelve portions. (First divide the log into three even parts, then cut each of the thirds in half, and finish by cutting each of those six pieces in half again.) Roll them into balls. Roll one side of each ball to form a little finger at least 4 inches (10 cm) long.

Place the fingers on a lined baking tray. Either brush or spray them with oil, then cover them with a damp tea towel and leave them until they become plump and fluffy, about 40 minutes.

Whilst the dough is rising, preheat the oven to 425°F (220°C) fan forced, or, for a non-convection oven, 455°F (235°C). In a bowl, whisk together your egg wash until there are no lumps of egg white remaining. When the dough has risen, lightly brush each finger with the egg wash, then place the tray in the oven for 10 to 15 minutes, or until the fingers are evenly golden and cooked through. Set them on a wire rack to cool.

Cut each finger bun horizontally, then fill it with your choice of jam or cream. Dust it lightly with icing sugar before serving.

Lucy's Loukoumades (Cypriot Donuts)

Makes 24 donuts

This recipe comes from one of our staff members, Lucy, who has been at Cakeboi since day one. Lucy is proud of her Greek heritage and often brings in mind-blowing Greek dishes she has cooked up at home.

When she whipped up a batch of her Loukoumades, we all went wild with joy. These little puffs of dough drenched in honey are wickedly addictive. This recipe is now one that I make at home for dinner parties.

1 small potato, peeled and diced

4 cups (960 ml) water

3⅔ cups (500 g) bread flour, divided

½ tsp salt

½ tsp sugar

1 tsp cinnamon

2 tsp (7 g) yeast

Honey Syrup

2 cups (480 ml) honey

3¼ oz (100 ml) water

1 tsp orange blossom water

4 cups (960 ml) vegetable oil, for frying

1 cup (240 ml) oil, to ensure the batter is nice and smooth

Place the potato in a small saucepan with the water, bring it to a boil over a high heat, then cook it for 5 minutes, or until softened. Remove the potato to a large mixing bowl, but do not discard the liquid. Set it to the side to cool.

Mash the potato with a fork until no lumps remain, then stir in the potato water. Add half of the flour and the salt, sugar, cinnamon and yeast, then mix everything together with your hands until a smooth paste is formed. Add the remaining flour and continue to mix until the batter comes together. Cover the dough with plastic wrap, then set it in a warm spot for 1 hour, or until doubled in size.

In the meantime, prepare your syrup. Place your honey, water and orange blossom water in a small saucepan and bring it to a boil, stir, then allow it to cool to room temperature.

Heat your oil to 355°F (180°C) over a medium heat. When ready, lightly fold the batter onto itself to ensure it is nice and smooth. Grasping a handful of batter in your hand, gently clench your fist until the batter pops out between your pointer finger and thumb. Use a spoon to scoop the dough off your thumb, then drop it into the heated oil. Lucy leaves her spoon in a cup of room-temperature oil between scoops to help release the dough from the spoon. Cook the donuts for 5 to 6 minutes, tossing continually, until they are light, golden and crisp.

Place the freshly cooked Loukoumades in a large bowl, then toss with the warm syrup.

7.
Inclusive Bakes

Food is something that we all enjoy, and at Cakeboi we put ingredients together in such a way that you experience creativity and innovation in every bite, regardless of your needs. I wanted to create an inclusive business that understands and values diversity. As with our ingredients, we recognize the individuality and value of every person.

Traditional baking has many techniques that produce delicious results. However, the vegan and gluten-free baking world is a different game. When I went vegan, there was little to look forward to in the baking world. Out of necessity, I rolled up my sleeves and started experimenting to vegan-ize some recipes.

When it comes to vegan or gluten-free baking, it is not just about substituting flour and dairy. The very nature of how ingredients work together is a delicate process.

I can now confidently say I have created some inclusive recipes that are so tasty they're ordered by non-vegan and gluten-tolerant customers. These include my Vegan Coconut and Raspberry Cake (page 147) and the Persian Love Cake (page 159). This is the vision I had, to create something that can be enjoyed by all, regardless of dietary needs. While other bakeries say no to your gluten-free or vegan dietary requirements, at Cakeboi, we say no problem.

Vegan Coconut and Raspberry Cake

Makes one 7-inch (18-cm) cake

Cakeboi's coconut and raspberry cake is inspired by the arrival of winter, a frosty façade that brings forth the warmth within. This cake is gift-wrapped in perfect white, as coconut snow rests upon the exterior. Cutting it ignites vibrant hues of raspberry red. This cake is light, soft and fresh like a snowflake.

2 cups (480 ml) coconut cream

4 tsp (20 ml) apple cider vinegar

¾ cup (180 ml) coconut oil

2 tsp (10 ml) vanilla extract

3¼ cups (400 g) self-rising flour

1½ cups (330 g) caster sugar

Pinch of salt

1 cup (128 g) frozen raspberries

1 cup (100 g) moist or dried coconut flakes

Icing

1½ cups (300 g) Copha or vegetable shortening

2¼ cups (500 g) vegan butter, at room temperature

3 cups (420 g) icing sugar mixture (page 14)

2 tsp (10 ml) vanilla extract

3 tbsp (50 g) raspberry Basic Berry Jam (page 30)

1 cup (100 g) moist coconut flakes

4 freeze-dried raspberries or ½ pint (1 punnet) fresh raspberries

Preheat the oven to 340°F (170°C), and grease and line two 7-inch (18-cm) baking tins. Pour the coconut cream and cider vinegar into a jug or another container that is easy to pour from and mix well, then set aside for 5 minutes. The mix may curdle, but just keep mixing it. Now add the coconut oil and vanilla to the jug, and mix until it is all well combined.

In a separate bowl, sift together the self-rising flour, caster sugar and salt. In three batches, mix the wet mixture into the dry ingredients using a spatula; don't use an electric mixer. Ensure that each addition is well incorporated. Finally, carefully fold through the raspberries and moist coconut flakes.

Evenly portion the cake batter into the lined cake tins, then bake on a center rack for 40 to 45 minutes, or until a toothpick inserted into the center comes out clean. Remove the cakes from the oven and let them rest in the tins for 10 minutes. Run a knife around the inside of the tins, then turn the cakes out and allow them to cool completely on a wire rack.

For the icing, heat the Copha in the microwave until softened and almost melted. Beat the vegan butter and the icing sugar mixture in a stand mixer on a medium speed until smooth. Turn the mixer to a low speed, pour in the melted Copha and vanilla, then mix until the icing is light and fluffy.

To assemble, horizontally cut each of the cakes into two layers, creating four layers in all. Place one layer on your cake stand and generously spread it with icing, then spread a tablespoon (15 ml) of jam over the icing. Repeat this process with the next two layers, then place the final layer on top and spread the remaining icing over the top of the cake and around the sides. Smooth the sides with a spatula, then sprinkle the coconut around the cake to give the snow effect. Then, decorate the top of the cake with crushed up freeze-dried raspberries or scatter with fresh raspberries.

Gluten-Free Almond, Blueberry and Coconut Tea Cake

Makes one 8-inch (20-cm) cake

1 scant cup (200 g) butter

1½ cups (180 g) almond meal

¾ cup (70 g) fine coconut (desiccated)

¼ tsp salt

1⅛ cups (250 g) caster sugar

4 eggs

2 tsp (10 ml) vanilla extract

¼ tsp almond extract

¼ cup (40 g) blueberries, fresh or frozen

2 tbsp (10 g) flaked almonds

Blueberry and coconut, what a delicious pairing! It was first introduced by an early staff member who loved baking this cake at home, and it was adapted to become a popular gluten-free option at Cakeboi. When you take a bite, you get a lovely soft texture bursting with a divine coconut flavor that pairs perfectly with the delicate sweet taste of blueberries. It's a perfect cake to go with a cup of tea or to have alongside breakfast or brunch.

(Note to American readers: We call this a tea cake but, yes, you can call it a coffee cake.)

This incredible cake is moist beyond measure and is sure to impress.

Preheat the oven to 355°F (180°C) and grease and line an 8-inch (20-cm) cake tin.

In a small saucepan on a medium heat, melt the butter, then remove it from the heat and allow it to cool until it is warm.

Bringing this cake batter together is fairly simple. Firstly, in a bowl mix together the almond meal, fine coconut, salt and caster sugar, then place it to the side. In a second bowl, mix together the eggs, vanilla extract, almond extract and melted butter. Bring the batter together by mixing the dry ingredients with the wet ingredients until well combined with no dry patches remaining.

Pour the batter into the prepared tin, then sprinkle the blueberries over it. Using a spoon, poke down some of the blueberries so that they sink below the surface. Finally, sprinkle the flaked almonds over the batter, then place the cake in the oven and bake for 45 minutes, or until a skewer test comes out clean.

Tips and Tricks: At Cakeboi, we have found that this cake is best after it is cooled in the fridge overnight. We don't remove it from the tin until the following morning.

Flourless Chocolate Cake

Makes one 8-inch (20-cm) cake

In this recipe, the heavenly richness of pure quality chocolate is perfectly balanced with bitterness to create an indulgent dark delight dusted in cocoa.

Watching this cake bake is deceptive. It rises high and plump, yet as it cools, it settles and deflates, leaving behind a crackled exterior. But remember, do not judge by appearance; a rich heart may be under a questionable coat.

At Cakeboi, this is a crowd favorite because people recognize it is flourless, not powerless!

¾ cup (170 g) unsalted butter

7 oz (200 g) dark chocolate, chopped

¼ cup (25 g) cocoa powder, sifted

6 large eggs, separated

⅔ cup (150 g) caster sugar

½ tsp salt flakes

1 tbsp (7 g) cocoa powder

Preheat the oven to 280°F (140°C) fan forced, or, for a non-convection oven, 310°F (155°C). Prepare an 8-inch (20-cm) springform baking tin by lining the base with baking paper. I feel that this cake rises the best if it is baked in an ungreased tin. So I use a springform tin, as this allows me to run a knife around the edge of the cake before popping the sides off.

To start the cake, melt the butter and chocolate in a microwave-safe bowl for 1 minute and 30 seconds. Stir the mixture to ensure all the chocolate is well melted. If lumps remain, return the bowl to the microwave for an additional 30 seconds. Allow to cool slightly, then stir in the cocoa powder and egg yolks.

With an electric mixer, whip the egg whites until they have doubled in size and become foamy. Turn the mixer to low and pour the sugar in a steady stream into the mixing egg whites, then continue to beat on a medium-high speed. The egg whites are ready if, when you remove the whisk, the meringue sits stiff and holds its shape.

Carefully fold the meringue through the chocolate mixture until a silky dark cake batter is formed. Pour the batter into the prepared baking tin, then sprinkle with salt flakes. Place the tin in the oven and bake for 40 minutes.

Allow the cake, in its tin, to cool to room temperature and then to set in the fridge. Run a knife around the edge of the cake before popping the sides off. Dust this cake with a rich dark cocoa powder before slicing.

Vegan Salted Chocolate and Miso Cookies

Makes 10–12 cookies

½ cup (120 g) vegan butter, at room temperature

⅔ cup (150 g) brown sugar

⅓ cup (80 g) caster sugar

2 tbsp (40 g) miso paste

2 oz (60 ml) oat milk, at room temperature

1⅔ cup (200 g) all-purpose flour

1 tsp baking powder

7 oz (200 g) vegan chocolate, chopped

Pinch of salt

"Miso—in cookies?" Yes, girl.

If the only thing you associate with miso is ramen, then this concept might sound weird. Rest assured, these heavenly, soft and thick cookies with melting chocolate chunks and a buttery texture have a hidden savory umami flavor. It is an even better combo than sea salt and caramel. The miso adds a wonderful, rich nuttiness to enhance this sweet chocolate chip cookie.

I didn't invent this idea, but I had some miso paste in my fridge and thought, why not experiment? It created the most amazing flavor. At first it is subtle, but it gradually builds and is balanced perfectly by the salt and chocolate.

This (vegan) miso chocolate chip cookie recipe is the best of so many worlds.

Firstly, preheat your oven to 355°F (180°C) fan forced, or, for a non-convection oven, 385°F (195°C). Prepare two baking trays lined with baking paper.

Place the butter, both sugars and miso paste in a large mixing bowl and beat with an electric mixer until it is thick and pale. This can also be done using a hand whisk.

Tips and Tricks: You can freeze any dough balls you don't want to use right away. Just slightly flatten the dough before freezing. When you're ready to bake them, pop them onto a tray, sprinkle with salt and bake them in the oven from frozen. They just take another 2 minutes.

Fold in the oat milk, flour, baking powder and vegan chocolate until they are fully incorporated. Using a tablespoon (15 g), measure out two spoonfuls of dough and then roll them into a ball. You should be able to get 10 to 12 cookie balls. Now space them over the two baking trays. Flatten the cookies with your hand or the back of a fork, then sprinkle them with salt.

Bake them in the oven for 15 minutes, or until they are golden around the edges. These cookies are done when the edges are crisp and the top is soft.

Try and resist the urge to eat these as they cool on the baking trays for 20 minutes.

Gluten-Free Vegan Lemon Poppy Seed Cake

Makes one 8-inch (20-cm) Bundt cake

Poppy seeds and lemon are a classic flavor combination that will surely please most cake eaters. This vegan lemon poppy seed cake is 100 percent gluten free, and it is deliciously moist, sweet and zesty with a little nutty crunch from the poppy seeds.

This cake is made with yogurt, which is why it is seriously moist. The yogurt also creates a beautifully flawless, dense crumb and a tangy flavor that complements the lemon juice.

1 lemon

¾ cup (180 ml) soy milk

1 tbsp (15 ml) apple cider vinegar

½ cup (120 ml) vegetable oil

1 tsp vanilla extract

1¼ cups (150 g) almond meal

1½ cups (190 g) buckwheat flour

Pinch of salt

2 tsp (10 g) baking powder

1 tsp baking soda

⅔ cup (150 g) caster sugar

½ cup (120 ml) coconut yogurt

1½ tbsp (13 g) poppy seeds

Glaze

2¾ cups (400 g) icing sugar

3 tbsp (45 ml) soy milk

1 tsp vanilla extract

1 tsp poppy seeds

Preheat the oven to 340°F (170°C) fan forced, or, for a non-convection oven, 365°F (185°C), and prepare a Bundt tin with spray vegetable oil and a light dusting of flour.

To start this cake, place your whole lemon in a small saucepan of boiling water and boil for 10 minutes. Remove the lemon and allow it to cool. Slice the lemon in half and remove any seeds. Then, with a blender, puree the whole lemon.

Pour the soy milk and cider vinegar into a large bowl, mix well, and set aside for 5 minutes. The mixture will curdle. Now add the oil and vanilla, then mix until it is all well combined.

Sift the almond meal and buckwheat flour, salt, baking powder and baking soda together into a large mixing bowl. Add the sugar and whisk it through. Slowly pour the soy milk and oil mixture into the dry ingredients whilst continually stirring. Lastly, mix through the pureed lemon, coconut yogurt and poppy seeds, then pour the batter into the prepared Bundt tin.

Bake for 30 minutes, or until a skewer inserted into the cake comes out clean. Rest the cake in the Bundt tin for 10 minutes, then invert it onto a wire rack for cooling.

For the glaze, whisk together the icing sugar, soy milk and vanilla in a large mixing bowl until a smooth glaze is formed. Pour the glaze over the cooled cake, then sprinkle with poppy seeds.

Makes 6 friands

⅔ cup (80 g) shelled pistachios or ground pistachio meal

⅓ cup (80 g) butter

½ tsp vanilla extract

3 egg whites

7 tbsp (50 g) buckwheat flour

¾ cup (100 g) icing sugar, plus extra for dusting

Fresh berries or figs

A fellow MasterChef *baking superstar, Genene, gave me this amazing recipe. I only tweaked her recipe by adding buckwheat flour. Buckwheat has the most beautiful grainy flavor. So let me introduce you to friands. Friands are delightful little cakes, invented by the French. They are light, buttery cakes often baked with decorative fresh fruit. It is the whipped egg whites that give these little cakes their lift, making them nice and light. The buckwheat flour and ground pistachios give the friands a rich nutty flavor and texture.*

These friands are not only gluten free but absolutely delicious!

Preheat the oven to 355°F (180°C) fan forced, or, for a non-convection oven, 385°F (195°C), and lightly spray the friand molds or a small muffin tray with vegetable oil.

If you're unable to source pistachio meal, just grind the pistachios by pulsing them in a food processor until they resemble almond meal, but not so long that they turn into a paste. Melt the butter in a small saucepan. (Sometimes I like to make brown butter, as per page 46. It does add a nice flavor, but this depends on time.) Once the butter is melted, strain it into a small bowl, stir in the vanilla, and set it aside.

Place the egg whites in a large mixing bowl, then whisk them with an electric mixer until they start to foam. Try not to over-whisk the egg whites, as you do not want them to be too thick.

Meanwhile, sift the buckwheat flour with the icing sugar into a bowl and then mix in the ground pistachios throroughly. Using a spatula, carefully fold these ingredients through the whisked egg whites. You want to retain as much air as possible when doing this.

Once all the dry ingredients have been folded in, add the butter and fold it into the batter. It will eventually mix in; just keep gently folding.

When the butter is fully incorporated, pour the batter into your chosen friand molds until they are three-quarters filled. Now push your selected fruit into the top of the batter.

Bake the friands for approximately 12 to 15 minutes, depending on the size of molds used. Once they are springy to the touch, cool them in their tray until they are at room temperature.

Tips and Tricks: This recipe is written for six because, like most baked goods, friands are best when freshly made. But if you have a dozen friand molds and a hungry horde, by all means double the quantities.

Genene's Gluten-Free
Friands

Persian Love Cake

Makes one 8-inch (20-cm) cake

2¼ cups (270 g) almond meal

½ cup (120 g) brown sugar

¾ cup (150 g) raw sugar

½ cup (70 g) buckwheat flour

7 tbsp (100 g) butter, at room temperature

¼ tsp salt

2 eggs

1⅓ cups (320 g) Greek yogurt

1 tsp vanilla extract

1 tsp rose water

½ tsp nutmeg

½ tsp cardamom

3 tbsp (30 g) icing sugar

2 tbsp (10 g) rose petals

5 freeze-dried or fresh raspberries

Once upon a time, a Persian woman was madly in love with a prince, so she baked him this cake filled with magical powers to make him fall for her. Honestly, she didn't need magic. This enchanting, fragrant rose cake is dense with brown sugar, lightened with yogurt, kissed by nutmeg and cardamom and topped with sprinkled rose petals. Trust me, the cake alone will win any heart—especially that of a gluten-free prince. Using raw sugar is a must; as the cake bakes, the sugar caramelizes, adding a depth of flavor and an addictive crunch.

You're going to fall in love with this cake!

To begin this recipe, preheat your oven to 355°F (180°C) fan forced, or, for a non-convection oven, 385°F (195°C). Grease an 8-inch (20-cm) springform baking tin and place a round cut of baking paper on the bottom of the tin.

To make the batter, use an electric mixer with a paddle attachment and combine your almond meal, brown sugar, raw sugar, buckwheat flour, butter and salt in a medium-sized mixing bowl. Ensure that all the dry ingredients are well coated in the butter, so that the mixture resembles breadcrumbs; this will help add crunch. Place one-half of this mixture in the bottom of your baking tin and lightly press to create an even layer of crust.

In a separate bowl, mix together the eggs, Greek yogurt, vanilla, rose water, nutmeg and cardamom to form a wet batter. Add the remaining half of the dry ingredients, then mix until well combined. Pour the batter into the baking tin, ensuring that the crust is covered, then place it in the oven.

Bake the cake for 30 to 35 minutes, or until the surface is lightly golden. Whilst the cake is still warm, carefully run a knife around the outside of the cake to release it from the sides, then gently pop the spring. Do not remove the cake from the base of the tin just yet. Transfer it to a wire rack to cool completely before decorating.

Once the cake is cooled, transfer it from the base to a serving dish, then dust it with icing sugar, followed by a sprinkling of rose petals. Finish with some broken-up freeze-dried raspberries.

Acknowledgments

There are a few people that I need to thank for helping me bring this book together. I had a very specific vision and style. At times I myself found the vision hard to translate, but these people understood it well. THANK YOU.

Firstly, my baking team. Brendan, my head baker at Cakeboi, thank you for having my back during the process of making this book, from looking after the shop if I was on a shoot to helping me decorate some of these cakes. Thank you.

The baking magician Genene Dwyer. Genene, you have been my backbone when writing these recipes. Translating Nan's old recipes has been a hugely wonderful experience, and I am so lucky to have been able to share it with you. Also, a special mention to Libby for helping me test out some of Nan's classic sponges.

My Cakeboi staff. Thank you for the dedication, commitment and love you bring to your jobs. You guys are the lifeblood of my business and are why customers line up every day.

My photography and design team of Luisa Brimble and Zoe Lonergan. Thank you for capturing the essence of Nan's and Cakeboi's recipes.

It goes without saying that I am forever grateful to my beautiful Page Street Publishing family. Thank you for seeing the potential in me to create this book. I have loved every moment of working with you all, and I thank you for allowing my dreams to come true.

Finally, thank you to my partner Dene. Each word in this book has had your eyes glance over it through late nights of edits and changes. I am grateful for the help and passion you have given to me to achieve this dream. I consider this book ours. Congratulations for it, thank you, I love you.

xxx

Reece

About the Author

Reece Hignell is a talented cake baker from Newcastle, Australia. He is known for his ambitious stints on *MasterChef Australia* and as the owner (or Bakerpreneur, as he puts it) of Cakeboi.

Baking has always been at the heart and soul of Reece's family, and it all started with his nan, Heather Bates. Heather was a fantastic baker who would bake for any occasion. She was locally renowned for her talent. Heather served her popular array of baked goods on weekends at her market stalls with Reece by her side.

Growing up, Reece would help his nan and mother prepare the cakes for the market. They would start baking early on a Saturday morning, first with the fruit cakes, followed by the butter cakes and finally the sponges. Reece would sit by their side and wrap each freshly iced cake, then box it ready for the next morning. These hours spent with his nan fueled a passion for baking that would follow Reece throughout his life.

When Reece was in his mid-twenties, he realized he was unhappy with his profession. He worked a secure job as a recruitment consultant, but the mundane nine-to-five role was not for him. Reece decided to apply for the popular reality cooking show *MasterChef*. Before he knew it, he was on a plane heading to Melbourne to compete in a world-renowned TV competition.

With two seasons of *MasterChef* under his belt, it was time for Reece to tackle the big world. In 2021, Reece opened his own bakery called Cakeboi. His bakery is a dedication to many things, including his memory of his nan's market stall, his love for all areas of baking and his passion for keeping old-school baking alive.

Reece spends most of his time working in his bakery, producing delectable recipes on Instagram and occasionally cooking on TV. Aside from that, he spends his downtime with his family made up of Dene, Monte, Carlo and Bernie.

Index